QUALITY
VENISON II

ALL NEW RECIPES
AND DEER

By Steve a...

In Appreciation

Let's take time here to give credit to those considerate individuals who have given us their time and talent and thus have made the self-publishing of this book possible. We first want to thank our Lord for giving us the health, time, and all of the following people so we could write *Quality Venison II*.

Special thanks goes out to gentleman artist, Jack Paluh, who allowed us the use of his beautiful, sold out print, "Monster Buck" on the cover of our book. We want to thank our talented and much loved daughter, Kelly, ("Star") for the deer illustrations that she drew for inclusion in our book, also. We want to thank Bob Mitchell, Editor of Pennsylvania Game News magazine for taking the time out of his busy schedule to give us article reprint permission, and then contributing both an article and recipe.

We also need to thank New York State Conservationist and North American Hunter magazines for article reprint permissions. Thanks go to Jim Zumbo, Terry Sullivan and illustrator Dimitry Schidlovsky for their permissions to reprint their interesting articles.

Lastly, but most importantly we want to thank Sheryn Jones and Merikay Jones of Cookbook Resources for all their on going assistance to make the self-publishing of our second Quality Venison cookbook possible. We are counting on them for their continued help with self-publishing, marketing, and sales advice.

1st Printing, 4,000 copies
2nd Printing, 5,000 copies
ISBN: 0-9662284-1-3

Copyright © 1999
Published by Loders' Game Publications, Inc.
PO Box 1615
Cranberry Township, Pennsylvania 16066
Phone: (724)779-8320 Fax: (724)779-9533

cookbook
resources.

541 Doubletree Drive
Highland Village, TX 75067
972/317-0245

Welcome Back To Our Country Kitchen

People who bought copies of our first book, *Quality Venison, Homemade Recipes & Homespun Deer Tales* have called or written with their praise for our book and its easy, tasty recipes. Well, we are cooking venison family style again, friends. There are over 150 new recipes and two new recipe categories; Cooking Venison Southern Style and Preparing Venison Marinades & Sauces for you to prepare using your quality cared for venison. As always, ENJOY!

MEMBER
PENNSYLVANIA OUTDOOR WRITERS ASSOCIATION

Our Inspired Acknowledgment

After completing our first cookbook, *Quality Venison, Homemade Recipes & Homespun Deer Tales,* we had extra articles to reprint with permission, extra recipes and real life deer tales from our hunting journal. We decided that if the Lord blessed the sale of *Quality Venison,* we would use this extra material to write a second book. This is it!

Our books are written to share our recipes and cooking styles, and we hope you enjoy sharing them with your family, friends and neighbors. God has blessed our publishing business with success, and we are donating a tithe amount of our book sales to Christian organizations and charities, that are helping to feed and care for the needy people in our community and around the world. It is our way of giving You thanks, Lord, for all You have done and will do for our family.

We hope you will remember to donate your own venison, on occasion, to churches and food banks that feed those in need. Venison from the whitetail deer is a gift from God and is meant to be shared.

CONTENTS

ON THE COVER: "MONSTER BUCK"

Limited Edition Print
painted by Jack Paluh

The noble pair was cautious and exceptionally mysterious as they broke from their marshy cover. Their appearance was only for an instant. His massive rack had exceeded any I had ever seen as it glowed in the evening light. He was the "Monster Buck" of which I had heard many tales. Then suddenly, as if they could hear the pounding of my heart, they just melted back into the thick wetland cover.

JACK PALUH, ARTIST

To the artist's eye, the outdoor world provides unlimited subject material for paintings. "My ideas are inspired while hunting and photographing outdoors," states Jack Paluh. "I observe colors, shapes and patterns of our ever changing seasons. My outdoor time enables me to watch animal behavior, study habitat and truly appreciate the amazing natural world that God has given us. Once I've gathered my information, I bring these ideas into my studio, where I compose it much like putting a puzzle together. As story telling has reinforced my past works, I hope to continue to tell a story with each piece I complete so my viewers share in these experiences.

Having successfully completed his **Living With the Land Theme**, the representation of the Hunting Skills of the Eastern Woodland Indians, Jack will continue to present Special Editions of these Native Hunters along with a New Study of our Traditional and Modern Day Hunters in Sporting Art Scenes. His art images will also include a variety of wildlife close to the hearts of his collectors.

"God has truly blessed me with a job that I love," expresses Paluh. "I encourage others to find their talents and develop them. It is my privilege and honor to share my artwork and to inspire others, especially our youth, to the wonders of the outdoors."

For more information on purchasing art prints by Jack Paluh, call 814-796-4400.

A Baker's Dozen New Deer Tales

Why Some of Us Deer Hunt

*I*nterest in hunting across America is waning when compared to ten years ago, but hunters keep spending more of their leisure income on hunting equipment, travel, food, lodging, licenses, etc. In a recent survey of its members the National Rifle Association found the greatest number of whitetail deer hunters are found in Pennsylvania and New York states by far. Other states where deer hunting is very popular are Wisconsin, Texas, Ohio, and Virginia respectively.

The reasons deer hunters gave for their interest in hunting were: 1) over half said enjoy the outdoors, 2) viewing wildlife, 3) sharing the experience with others, 4) hunting for venison, and lastly, hunting for a trophy. But there are a great deal of us deer hunters who hunt for the exercise and the challenge of taking our deer of either sex; in any kind of weather, too. Nutritious venison from the white tail deer has always been appreciated on our family's dinner table. A good deerless hunter at the end of the season doesn't mind giving credit to the

Continued on page 8

quarry when they have to go the next year without their venison. There is always next season to even the score.

When deer hunting is done right with safety first and respect for the whitetail, other hunters, and landowners' rights taken into consideration, every deer season is full of "fond" memories.

NOW LET'S GO READ SOME REAL DEER TALES . . .

DEER HUNTERS NEVER COME HOME EMPTY HANDED

It is all set. I just got off the phone with a hunting partner and we would be hunting the last day of the primitive weapons season together on Saturday. Mark would use his bow and I would be hunting with my muzzleloader for an either sex deer. I was deerless so far and it was nice to see that even at the end of the season we still had the desire to keep hunting for a possible trophy (mountable buck) and the venison for our family or charity.

As usual the alarm clock scared me at 5 A.M. when it went off, but by now getting dressed and going down the road in thirty minutes or less was a routine. Oh, do not forget to take that apple for a refreshing morning snack. At seven A.M. it was just breaking daylight when we separated. Mark would be hunting one ridge and I would be on the ridge on the other side of the road. We would meet back at the vehicle at about noon to compare notes or swap deer tales, hopefully. Maybe help the other to get his deer to the road for the happy trip home.

Honest, I was not in the woods five minutes when after not thinking a thing about it, I blew my nose. Next thing I saw out of the corner of my eye was the white of a deer's tail wagging as it bounded away from me at about seventy yards. Already a mistake, I thought, since I did not get off a shot. Is this a bad omen?

Picking out a tree for my tree seat was easy. The creek below was shallow enough to wade with a deer if I had to cross it and there was plenty of fresh deer tracks and dropping to make me feel confident about hunting only half way up the ridge.

As daylight approached wild turkeys could be heard "talking" to each other. You know, gobbling, clucking, putting, tree calling, etc. So for about an hour I was treated to a turkey serenade until they all flew down to start their morning feeding on the ridge above and away from me.

By mid-morning I had only seen one huge red fox squirrel and watched a flock of Canadian geese fly over the very top of this ridge. The temperature was a comfortable 30 degrees or so and for once there was not a trace of wind. So I could see and hear fine, but the deer did not make their presence known. They must be hiding because they know of my reputation as a deer hunter and somehow they knew I was hunting here this morning. That is a perfectly rational excuse for my not seeing a deer all morning, isn't it?

The morning passed quickly and just before releasing my tree seat my mind wandered further. Yes, the nice thing for a deer hunter is they never come home empty handed or without getting something. Most of the time the little thoughts and feelings you experience while outdoors are retained memories. Those outdoor memories become a significant part of who we are over the years that we hunt deer, small game, and waterfowl. It just does not matter what game brings us into the outdoors. Being outdoors is to be appreciated and taking a deer or any wild game just makes any day's outdoor experience even more special year after year.

A CASE OF SOUTHERN HOSPITALITY

I luckily made a new friend the summer we moved to Mississippi because of another job promotion. I say luckily because as an outside account manager I traveled central Mississippi to meet with accounts and I did not spend any time in our local area. So I had trouble meeting guys to hunt with before the gun deer season opened.

My new friend was J. D., owner of the local sporting goods store and bait shop. J. D. had lived in Meridian, Mississippi all his life and he spent most of it hunting and fishing so he was certainly in the right line of work.

I hunted with J. D. two times of the six outings I made to hunt for a buck, but so far I had not even seen a buck. The next time I saw J. D. I learned he took a respectable six point buck. I congratulated him and he asked if I had any luck. When I told him no, not yet, I guess he felt sorry for me because he knew our family's appreciation for venison. He then offered to take me to his special spot when the doe season came in if I did not have my buck already. Hey, you do what it takes to put venison in the freezer, even if that means taking a legal doe.

Well, I did not get a buck, despite the long Mississippi white-tail season, so with the buck season ending and the three day doe season beginning on Saturday, it was time to drop by J. D.'s shop. Good old J. D. was glad to see me and he would keep his promise after all about hunting together to fill our doe tags come Saturday. At 5:30 A.M. we were to meet at his store and deer hunt private property that he had permission to hunt. J. D. said he had taken deer there before because of the more than helpful land owner. Despite days of cold, lonely, sometimes boring buck hunting with no luck, I was anxious for Saturday to come. Hey, I have hunted hard for a buck and now if I am blessed with a doe, at least it will give me some great tasting, nutritious venison for my family and me, so let's do it.

No problem getting up at 4:45 A.M. Saturday morning. When I arrived at J. D.'s shop he was there in his truck as usual. He made room on the seat for my hunting coat and my 30-06 deer rifle went between my legs, and my tree seat went on the floor.

After driving nearly an hour, during which we had complained about, and then solved most of this country's problems, we pulled into a farmer's dirt driveway. Before leaving the truck there was the all important "hunt game plan" to discuss. We decided we would both sit still all morning in the woods watching for deer along a huge soybean field. This hunting position made me glad I had my Remmington Model 760 scoped deer rifle. J. D. had a scoped Winchester Bolt Action 270. We were ready for a long range shot if necessary.

It was barely light enough to see as we walked a dirt road the twenty minutes or so it took to get "way back" to what was supposed to be a choice hunting spot, if you believed J. D. J. D. wished me luck and mentioned again if either of us get a doe, tag it and come and get the other guy, otherwise he would be back to get me at lunch time.

When dawn came, it was under thirty degrees and cloudy. My tree seat was a big help to keep me staying comfortable, warm and nearly motionless, as usual, but with each passing hour of not seeing any deer, my optimism was diminishing. Only an occasional rifle shot could be heard, too, all morning. My mid-morning Snickers bar perked me up for a little while. At around 11:30 A.M. J. D. came back for me. He had not seen any deer, either, but he had wished the wild turkey was is season. He saw two different flocks because one had eight birds and two hours later he saw a flock of sixteen birds come forging through.

Back at the truck we had a sandwich and coffee. Jim, the farm owner, stopped work long enough to say hello and remind J. D. that we should do a mini deer drive in the wooded hedgerow that divided two soybean fields on the other side of the road. OK, we agreed we would do it before sitting again on watch later in the afternoon.

On our mini drive J. D. wanted me on the edge of the field looking down into the woods at the direction J. D. would be coming from. He gave me a thirty minute head start to set up well in front of him before he started driving. J. D. was to make noise to scare the deer ahead of him and the noise would also help me shoot safely if a shot presented itself at an on-coming doe.

About the time I was thinking, no deer and where is he, I heard brush breaking and a doe flew out of the woods and ran across the field before I could shoulder my rifle. By the time I could aim she was out of range. Then I heard more brush breaking, I still had my rifle up and a doe appeared exactly where the first doe came out fifty yards away. It made a big mistake by stopping on the edge of the field to see if it could see the other doe before taking off after it. That careful pause allowed me time enough to squeeze off one shot into the deer's lung, shoulder area. The deer went down the instant the rifle fired and never moved. A clean one shot kill just like we all want them to be.

Thirty minutes later J. D. congratulated this happy deer hunter. I offered to share the venison with him but with his country charm he declined, saying he had venison and he was glad to have helped me get mine. After carefully field dressing the deer J. D. carried my tree seat and rifle and I had the proud job of getting my venison to the truck.

"Too bad all deer hunts do not end this way," I said to J. D. "Hey now, if they did, it would not be long before anti-hunters would be calling our sport deer shooting not deer hunting. Then there are a few deer hunters out there, too that would not respect the deer for its venison if it was easily accessible. We would not want that, would we, Steve?"

You know, he was certainly right on target there .....

WAS IT POOR EYESIGHT OR A "HIDDEN" BRANCH!

In 1987 it was good fortune that occurred to our family when a job promotion caused us to relocate within a five hour drive of home in upstate New York a few months before the New York gun deer season. Like we had done years ago, we made plans to visit our relatives on the weekend before Thanksgiving so I would be able to hunt whitetail deer with the opening of the season on that first Monday. Like old times, I would be hunting the Arliss farm in Clyde, NY with their family and the "crew."

I brought my 50 caliber Thompson Center muzzleloader with me and my shot gun. I was looking forward to taking my first deer with my smoke pole. With tags for both buck and a doe it did not matter which I took. Venison was the meat that mattered.

On opening Monday morning, as it turned out I got three shots with my Ithaca automatic 12 gauge at a small deer. Chippy shot and missed. I saw its small spikes too late as it flew by me and I shot too quickly. Buck fever, I guess! You know, not thirty minutes later another buck crossed the open corn field behind Larry's house, and Chippy had to shoot 12 times to hit the 6 point once. Man, his eye sight is gone. I thought if he does not get glasses this next season I doubt he will be able to see well enough to hit a deer at any range. Over the years he has been the luckiest guy I know when it comes to deer hunting. Buck or doe, it does not matter. They run him over all season long. Chip was a good shot before his eyes went bad. Got to give him credit there.

On the last day of my four day New York deer hunt I got a one shot opportunity to fill my doe tag with my muzzleloader. When daylight came I was sitting between two deer trails that I was famil- iar with. I had taken shots at deer from here in years past. The weather was calm and comfortable - around 25 degrees. With no deer sightings the first hour after daylight I settled in for an ex- pected four hour watch until lunch time.

Suddenly, three single shotgun slugs were fired near my stand. I caught a glimpse of three doe running scared across a field but angling toward me. I raised and cocked the muzzleloader. I was following the deer in my sights and then when they were in range, I automatically stopped my gun swing and aimed the muzzleloader in a clearing between the trees. When the first deer crossed the clearing I would fire on the deer's vital area broadside. Good plan ...... Yes and no!

Boom, the muzzleloader sounds off and the black powder cloud made it very hard to see if the deer went down. After a brief wait I searched for the deer or blood trail, but no luck. I returned to my stand and reloaded. It was hard to figure how I had missed the shot.

Recalling exactly the scenario a few times, I noticed a cut branch coming off a tree twenty feet in front of me and in the exact line of my fire at the deer. The branch deflected my bullet. Good effort but no venison for the family this year, but it was my own fault.

THE BUCK THAT GOT AWAY ...

The opening day of the New York shotgun deer season was only a week away when our Regional Sales Manager announced a mandatory two day meeting would be held in Washington the first two days of the season. Outwardly I acted politically correct, like, oh I did not have any other plans, but inside I felt sick. Being off deer hunting the opening week was a tradition with me for years, no matter what state I was living in. But on the other hand, my family had to eat and pay our bills so I would have to make the needed adjustments to my deer hunting plans, and attend the sales meeting.

That night I discussed this change in our vacation plans with my family. We decided to leave for vacation and my deer hunting after the sales meeting and after our daughter came home from school. My wife and daughter would visit family and friends while I hunted deer with our crew on the Bill Arliss farm in Clyde, NY.

I showed up at the farm house at 6:00 A.M. really excited about being on my first deer hunt of the year. As I remember I had not taken a buck in three years and the venison that was in our freezer was long ago eaten up. Over coffee I learned only four bucks and six doe were taken off the farm in the first three days of the season. This now being Thanksgiving morning, lots of hunters would be out and moving deer so everyone felt confident about our crew's chances of a successful morning hunt. Then we would spend the remainder of Thanksgiving day with our families.

Both Rog and Larry Arliss had deer stand locations in mind for me. I chose to be in a tree at the north end of their corn field that borders the famed so called big swamp. Unfortunately, because I had an out of state deer license I was not selected for a permit to take a doe this season. As I was climbing into the tree stand I thought, "you are shooting bucks only, Steve, so you better shoot straight if you get a shot at your buck. It may be your only chance to get your venison."

By day light shotguns could be heard regularly near and far as area hunters set their sights on an abundant deer population in this central New York area. Naturally, much alfalfa and corn is grown to feed the region's dairy herd so the whitetail deer are very well fed. All hunters here agree this makes for some delicious venison, either from a buck or doe for the family's dinner table.

Earlier this fall I had read the articles on Boning Your Deer, and The Way to Quality Venison and I had learned a lot so I was going to follow their tips on proper field dressing care, and boning out my own deer for the first time, provided I was fortunate enough to take my buck. (Those great how to articles are included in our first venison cookbook). When I mentioned this plan to Roger Arliss he said good for you. There is nothing to it and you will like having the ability to custom cut your venison for special meals, and butchering it yourself saves money, too! They had been hand processing their deer on the farm for many, many years. With this settled, I got back to thinking hunting.

This tree stand was not much help for protection from a 15 to 20 MPH wind and with the temperature below 20 degrees, this morning's watch would eventually be a cold one. My opening day (to me) optimism was beginning to freeze up by mid-morning. Suddenly three shotgun slugs were fired from over the ridge. They were from the Welch family camp so I got my shotgun ready to fire if they moved a buck to me for a shot. I heard the deer running before I saw it. At first look it did not have horns but I aimed and waited for it to come closer. When the nice size doe passed at 40 yards I could only let it go. NO TAG! Darn ...

By noon time I welcomed the warming walk back to the car and I was wondering if we (our crew) had enough of us left to put on one or maybe two small deer drives before going home for Thanksgiving dinner?

Up at the Arliss farm house the group was planning two drives behind the house before calling it a day. On the first drive I was a pusher and one doe was taken by Johnny, one of the watchers. On the second drive I was a designated watcher. Yes, I was excited.

Bill Arliss stayed with our crew in the pick up trucks to be able to place six of us watchers along the end of the woods near the camp. Once in position it did not take long before shots were fired. That did not guarantee there was a buck in there, but I got more excited ... I checked my five shot Ithaca Deerslayer shotgun and stared up the pasture wood line with the camp to my left. Twenty minutes later three, four shotguns fired. Then three doe bounded into the field and turned. Hesitating they decided not to cross it, instead they were running right at me. I slid behind the tree for a few seconds and then took another look at them to inspect for hidden spike horns.

No, no horns, but behind them now was a buck. Again, I eased behind the tree to wait for my shot. Easing out, when I could not wait any longer caused the buck to turn away and run across the field. It was now or never. I fired, at forty yards missed, fired and hit the buck on the shoulder. It almost fell but recovered and my nervous third and last slug missed.

Wow, I was mad that I had missed my first and third shots. That second slug hit the buck good as indicated with the amount of blood sign where the buck nearly fell. After the drivers arrived, Roger helped me trail the wounded buck. It was starting to rain so we could lose the blood trail if we waited for the buck to expire on its own before trailing it. We decided to stay on the blood trail until we found the buck or ran out of sign.

How we lost the blood trail and where that buck went to get away we do not know. We searched for 2-1/2 hours for the deer. Rog had never lost a deer hit that hard before, and it was to be my first. I did not want to talk about it at our Thanksgiving meal that I was late for. Talk about disappointed, but so was my wife, Gale and family.

In the years since losing that first deer I have learned to practice shooting more, and never be over confident in shot placement. So, although our family went without venison that year, thank God I have not hit and lost a deer since then. I know there are hundreds of hunters each year who accidentally wound and lose a whitetail deer. They learn from their mistakes and do what it takes out of respect for the whitetail to see to it they do not wound and lose another deer.

I do not know of any hunter that will tell the deer tale of the one that was hit but got away because it certainly is a bad memory that you are not proud to talk about. While I deserve to go without venison this year, my wife won't like it. She would much rather eat and prepare nutritious venison for our family's dinner table than eat BEEF!!

FRIENDS SHARE THE HARVEST

Earlier I told you the deer tale about the circumstances surrounding my losing my first buck because of poor shot placement. Now let me tell you the rest of the story.

After losing my buck on Thanksgiving afternoon I was disappointed, to say the least, but I was up-and-at-em Friday morning with a renewed sense of purpose. Rog Arliss met me at Bill and Ella's farm house just after 6 A.M. Rog had a plan for us to hunt a small patch of woods near the swamp. While working the area a few weeks earlier he saw deer using a trail three days in a row sometime during the morning. Rog wanted us to be on stand 150 yards apart with him hunting in one direction and I would be watching the trail from the other.

Upstate New York had a very wet fall that year so there was a lot of water everywhere near my watch location. Thank God for well insulated, rubber boots and my tree seat, I thought, as I rested my shotgun on a tree limb and stood waiting for first light.

Shotgun fire could be heard near and far as daylight came. The close shotgun fire meant either members of our hunting crew or the Welch family were trying to fill their deer tags for a supply of next year's venison. The longer I waited and watched for a movement that could have been my buck the more my mind reminded me of my yesterday's missed opportunity to take my buck with a clean one shot kill. With the temperature in the low teens and the snow flakes flying once again, I wished it were warm enough to be raining and not snowing.

By 9:30 A.M. the chill was getting to me and I wanted to move around and warm up. Before I made that decision, one, two, three shotgun slugs were fired from Rog's direction. In anticipation I waited to see if any deer would use the trail to pass by me "on the fly." I did not see a deer but my hunting interest was certainly peaked for the remainder of my morning watch.

At 10:30 A.M. with the New York winds picking up and the snow piling up, Roger came to pick me up. Rog wanted help getting his seven point buck out to a farm road where we could get at it with a pick up truck. I congratulated Rog because it was the first buck for him in several years, I know. Seems like he can't stop working long enough to hunt. It had our area's typical small rack, but it was a well fed deer, too. He would get at least fifty pounds of venison from him and his family.

By noon we had Rog's buck hanging up at the farm, so we broke for lunch and listened to the deer tales from some of the other party members. Paul Welch had also taken a 10 point buck that morning and Ella, Rog's mom, filled her doe tag. Paul's 10 point was the largest deer I ever saw taken on the farm. I had high hopes of filling my buck tag while on watch that afternoon, because time was running out. Too bad we did not have more of our hunting party members staying around so we could put on a drive or two, I thought.

After some of Ella's venison stew and an hour's rest, Rog, his brother, Larry, and I were headed in different directions for our afternoon's deer watch. As the day had gone along the temperature seemed to be dropping and now snow was again falling. It would be a pretty afternoon to be outdoors once I donned the extra insulated vest I remembered to bring.

No matter how hard I wished for a buck to come within shot-gun slug range in the hours before sunset, no buck appeared. Yes sir, it seemed our family would go without venison this year because sunset meant the end of my deer hunt. In the morning I would be driving the family back to our home in Lansdale, Pennsylvania.

Later I met Rog back at the farm house. He knew how disappointed I was over losing my first buck and how much we appreciated venison. He said, "stop by tomorrow morning with your family to visit before heading home, would you?"

The next morning we packed up and said good-by to my parents. Within the hour my wife, daughter and I were with the Arliss family having one last cup of coffee at the farm.

Rog said he wanted to show me something, so I followed him out to the barn. He showed me his skinned buck and said, "here, take it home, you and your family love venison." "What?" I said. He said, "I still have a doe tag to fill over two weeks of hunting." "Rog, if you really want me to have it, I will gladly take it, but ...." "No problem, I want you to have it."

Until now I had always had my deer butchered. He showed me how to remove the venison back straps and quarter the deer so it would fit into the two Coleman coolers I brought along. I had planned to bone-out my buck if I had gotten one, so now when I got home I would follow a boning guide to bone-out Rog's buck. That very boning guide has served me well over the years and is a valuable part of our first venison cookbook.

Hands on quality control of your venison from field to freezer is essential. Venison that is boneless, trimmed - no fat left on the meat, age controlled, and double freezer wrapped, is nutritious and will be delicious when carefully prepared like you would the finest beef.

Thanks again, Rog for generously sharing your venison. You know how much my family and I appreciated it.

"JUST DO IT"

Mother Nature more often than not will usually provide the most inclement and unpredictable weather for deer hunters in the northeast during that all important opening week of the deer gun season. This year the five hour drive with my family from Philadelphia to upstate New York was windy and rainy, so the miserable weather would once again stand in the way of my bagging a deer. Fortunately, this season I had my out-of-state buck tag and I was lottery chosen to receive a doe tag also.

As usual my family visited with Mom and Dad and other relatives the week-end before opening Monday of the shotgun only deer season. The lake effect weather of on and off rain with strong winds continued all day Sunday and well past my bed time. But I am a diehard deer and duck hunter so no matter what the fowl weather conditions awaited me; you just dress for it and tough it out.

Opening morning I was up with my Dad who was preparing to start his day at our restaurant at 5 A.M. I followed my Dad to Loder's Restaurant for a big breakfast and to tell deer tales with other deer hunting friends who would be having breakfast there, too.

After a huge breakfast (I never eat that much ...) we wished each other good luck and departed to our favorite deer hunting spots. I was one of the early arrivals at the Arliss farm but Bill and Ella were having coffee and their sons Fred, Rog, and Larry were soon to arrive. I am always excited about the opening day of the gun deer season but the Arliss family is very practical and experienced and they were disappointed with the fowl weather. The odds are in the deer's favor in weather like this, they said, because many fair weather deer hunters, opening day or not will not be in the hunting party or will not be there for long. The more hunters out hunting and moving deer the better the success rate for all of us to fill our tags.

Roger suggested I take my opening two to three hour watch at the north end of the big alfalfa field and he would not be far away. At daylight with the temperature below forty degrees, it was raining and the winds were howling between 30-35 mph, so there was not the usual frequent shotgun fire that is so common on opening day of deer season.

Rog came back to my ground blind to get me at 9 A.M. It had been raining hard for half an hour and he did not have good rain gear. We went back to the farm and were surprised to see only a few members of our hunting group were out to hunt. We did not even have enough hunters to do any successful deer drives. Over the next few hours the weather did not improve at all so I finally had to go back home to pick up some dry clothes.

After I returned to the farm I had some of Ella's venison and vegetable soup, donned my rain parka with a hood, grabbed my shotgun and slugs and headed out for a three hour watch for my deer. I never saw a deer on watch. At 5 P.M. I returned to the car and opened the trunk to put my shotgun away. The bolt had frozen up and I could not eject the three slugs. "Put it in the trunk," I thought and "I will take it inside the house to warm it up, then I can clear the magazine."

That made sense but because I was thinking about getting into warm, dry clothes and eating a hot meal when I arrived home, I forgot to take my shotgun inside to clear it.

The next morning I was at the Arliss farm at 6 A.M. After coffee and deer tales I was off to set up on watch for two or three hours. The overnight temperatures had fallen into the teens but the winds persisted, and it was raining again. "It is only the second day of the deer season, and I have two deer tags, so rough weather or not it is time to hunt." That was my thought just prior to opening my trunk to get my semi-automatic shotgun. But then reality hit me when I saw the shotgun and realized the action must be still frozen. "Well, if I have to fire it the first slug will fire and maybe the blast will knock the frozen action free." Right!

So with daylight minutes away I closed the trunk and headed off to a ground blind location in the triangle hoping to take my either sex deer with one well placed 12 ga. slug. The gun may not fire again ..... After enduring over two hours of cold and windy weather, the snow was flying, too, I was getting cold and I had to move. So I did some deer still hunting for an hour or so.

Out of no where a deer broke out of the woods and was going to cross the corn field near Larry's house. Then there were two other doe following it on the run. While I was deciding whether or not I would try this rather long shot a buck appeared at the wood line. It paused to decide if he really wanted to follow those doe crossing an open field or back track. Without thinking about it I dropped to one knee to steady the shotgun. The buck had started across the field but when I knelt down it stopped in mid-stride and stared through a wooded hedgerow right at me. It always amazes me how well a deer can see and especially see a hunter's slightest movement.

Having a standing still broadside shot at the buck's vital lung, shoulder neck area I eased off the safe and pulled the trigger. There was a click but never fired. The gun never fired because the firing pin was frozen up, and it never impacted the slug to make it fire.

That buck was laughing at this hunter after it reached the other side of the corn field and joined up with the other three doe. To say the least, I was disappointed with myself.

With no choice, I took my frozen shotgun back to the farm and warmed it up by placing it near the wood stove in the barn for an hour or two. After some of Ella's liver and onions with hot coffee I was ready to hunt and encouraged several of our crew not to give up for the day. By 2 P.M. I was on my tree seat but this time even further into the triangle woods. Looking at new woods and trails would keep me optimistic and sharp. The on again, off again rain and the continuous high winds made for a challenging hunt. If the temperature were not at about 40 degrees it would have been an even tougher deer watch but I had been there before. You just do it to get your deer.

Just after 4 o'clock with afternoon daylight waning, I spotted movement about 60 yards away. It was a nice size lone deer and it was feeding slowly on a trail coming toward me so I sat absolutely motionless. At about 40 yards when the big doe would be eating and not looking, I slowly positioned my shotgun for a shot. At 25 yards I eased off my gun safety quietly and fired at the deer's vital lung area. It was a clean one shot kill. I felt the proud accomplishment that comes from toughing out bad weather and overcoming a frozen shotgun mistake to secure some quality venison for my family and me. It was time to tag the deer, field dress it, and go get the pick-up truck! Thank you, Lord, for the venison this whitetail deer will provide for my family.

"KEEP YOUR POWDER DRY"

"Keep your powder dry," is a very old outdoor saying that must have been coined when early firearms all used black powder to ignite and fire their muskets and pistols. It emphasized how it was vital to keep your black powder dry if you expected your firearm to do its job and fire when called upon.

With the Pennsylvania gun deer season approaching it was time to squirrel hunt while I was deer scouting a piece of private property where I was given permission to hunt. So on Saturday morning I was up at 5 A.M. getting some coffee, toast and fruit before I left at 5:30 A.M. The property I would hunt was an hour away at highway speed so this hunt was not a walk in the park.

Daylight was just coming as I was loading my 12 ga. double barrel shotgun with low base squirrel and rabbit loads. Slowly and as quietly as I could step I eased through the woods listening and looking for that first squirrel amongst the deer sign that was beginning to become plentiful.

By mid-morning the sun was shining brightly and I had bagged two squirrels. There was plenty of deer sign and I managed to get a good look at a four point buck. By lunch time I had done enough scouting so I planned to come back here on the opening day of the gun deer season.

Since I was successful in taking a doe in New York the week of Thanksgiving I already had our family's supply of next year's venison, so when the Pennsylvania deer season opened the following Monday I wanted to challenge myself and I would attempt to take my first buck with my Thompson Center .50 caliber muzzleloader. My muzzleloader is a percussion cap engaged. That means it is not legal in the state of Pennsylvania during the flintlock muzzleloader only primitive weapon season but it is certainly legal during the gun deer season.

After returning from my successful shotgun only deer hunt in New York I carefully hand processed my doe into venison steaks, roasts, chops; even made my own venisonburger and sausage. Yes sir, we will have plenty of quality cared for venison to use in many different recipes. Thank you, Lord.

Somehow I even made time to target shoot my muzzleloader one more time because I had not shot it in months and I wanted to feel confident in my shooting. After target shooting I cleaned it like usual, without thinking anything about it. I placed it upright in my gun cabinet until I would use it on opening day.

Sunday night I made all the preparations for my morning muzzleloader hunt. Uncharacteristically, the weather was supposed to be mild, over 30 degrees at dawn and warming into the high 40's, so this helped me be even more eager to hunt for a buck after daylight. I was up at 5 A.M., left home by 5:30 A.M. so I could get into the woods well before daybreak.

After loading my muzzleloader with 100 grains of pyrodex and a .50 caliber round ball, I grabbed my accessories or possibles bag, my rifle and trusty tree seat, and headed up a four-wheeler trail leading to the top of the small ridge. About half way up is where a creek runs parallel to the ridge and that is where I had seen the four point buck three weeks earlier. The stream was brush lined on either side of it so it gave deer some protection when moving along the ridge. If there were a tree large enough in diameter to hold me on my tree seat that is exactly where I should hunt for a close shot on an unsuspecting buck.

Just after daylight I found a good tree for the tree seat and it importantly gave me three fairly good shooting lanes through the brush. It was not thirty minutes after being set up that I detected movement in the brush. It was time to use my straight line capper to cap and arm my muzzleloader. There was still some movement in the brush and it was moving in toward me as I slowly and quietly as possible cocked the muzzleloader.

When I could see the shape of the deer's body through the brush I began to slowly raise the muzzleloader. The same time I saw the deer was a buck, he sighted me. I knew I could not blink an eye much less move, but I was in great position if the buck moved into the nearest shooting lane. I held my breath; then let it out real slow while aiming in order to relax. When I had a good shot at the buck's chest area, I pulled the trigger.

The percussion cap popped but the muzzleloader did not fire. To say I was shocked is an understatement .... I was confident with this weapon and had not had a misfire in several years. Luckily the young four point never moved but was on high alert. Slowly I used the straight line capper to cap the rifle again after cocking the hammer. The buck moved a little but I had raised my muzzleloader into shooting position and was squeezing off a second shot as it moved into a brushless area. The cap popped but again the muzzleloader did not fire.

The buck started to run off as I cocked and capped my rifle a third time. For some reason the buck looked back at me at 50 yards and stopped. I had enough time to aim again through light brush at his vital lung area and fired a third time. Once again the cap popped but it did not set fire to the powder and the muzzleloader did not go off. This time the buck had seen enough and it ran off. That was one lucky buck because all three shots should have been a one shot kill.

To say that I was mad at my muzzleloader was an understatement. I felt like "giving it to the woods" and going home without it. I had to fire three more caps to get it to finally fire. I knew I had blown my buck opportunity because a second shot at a buck in the same day would not be likely. The weather was beautiful, though and there was plenty of shooting all around me so far so after calming down I reloaded my muzzleloader and hunted until noon.

Moral of the story: Always dry fire a cap on your muzzleloader prior to hunting with it to assure it will fire. After cleaning my muzzleloader a day or two before hunting, water or oil or both must have collected in the powder area of the barrel when it was placed upright in the gun cabinet after cleaning. The water or oil dampened the powder enough to cause my ill-timed misfires. It also cost me a first buck with my old smoke pole, but maybe next year . . . . .

First Deer Taken
With "A Smoke Pole"

Prior to the 1990 New York gun deer season I was a bit under-the-weather and I was afraid of my not being able to hunt on opening day, which is always the Monday before Thanksgiving. But as the season approached as usual I could not keep deer hunting out of my mind. With an expensive out-of-state license purchased months earlier that gave me both buck and doe tags, I decided I was going to hunt, somehow ....

With the uncertainty of the length of my deer hunt, my wife and daughter decided to stay home this time and plan for us to have Thanksgiving together at home in Philadelphia, when I returned. If I could tough out three days of deer hunting it could mean having venison for us to enjoy all of next year if I were successful.

The first Monday and Tuesday of the shotgun deer season were very quiet. It must be the plentiful doe tags for the past couple of years meant hunters were taking more deer and the herd size in the Lockpit area near Clyde, NY was decreasing. The first two days I had not seen a buck. So far I saw only three doe cross a large corn field on the Arliss farm well out of range for my shotgun's deer slugs. Paul and Fred took bucks and two other doe were also taken. I remained optimistic that sick or not if I was out there all day Wednesday I could get a chance to put some venison in our family's freezer.

On Wednesday, the third day of the season, my Dad woke me up with him at 5:30 A.M. As usual he was preparing to go to our restaurant and feed some of our area's hungry deer hunters. I can remember feeling so weak and disappointed that I did not want to go into the restaurant to face the traditional friendly kidding from my other hunter friends because I did not have my deer already. So I went directly to the Arliss farm and met up with only a handful of our usual deer hunting crew. I learned some of the guys did not have any vacation to use and some others were hunting elsewhere this first week.

Whatever Works! By 6:30 A.M. I was off with a flashlight and slug loaded Ithaca Deerslayer shotgun, making my way into a tree stand at the north end of the big alfalfa field. Years past I had regularly seen deer from the stand but so far I had taken only one deer from it. Hey, I thought, maybe today will be the day that I put a fatal deer slug into that trophy racked buck that I saw three years earlier. For once the New York weather was actually mild so the watch would be a comfortable one; that is a switch . . . . . .

The sun rose, it was clear and bright; the sound of shotgun fire could be heard regularly all morning. It was a beautiful day to be outdoors and to be deer hunting, too, made my experience even better. Though I prayed "Lord let me take my deer today, it is the last day of my hunt," at least 100 times by noon, I still did not see a deer. Even my deer call of whispering "here deer, here deer," did not work .... but maybe it will someday.

Lunch time I drove home to get something to eat and get a nap. I was sick and exhausted and did not know when I went to sleep if I could hunt later that afternoon or not. After lunch I got an hour's rest and the weather was just beautiful when I woke up, so I had to hunt. To make the last hunt more enjoyable I decided to leave my shotgun home and try again to take my first deer with my 50 caliber muzzleloader. By three P.M. I was back at the Arliss farm to check in with them about my deer watch plans, so no other hunter would mistakenly pass by my stand location before dark.

Now I felt I should not be disturbed when I took my last two hour deer watch again from the tree stand at the end of the big alfalfa field. It was a beautiful, sunny day as I left the car for a short hike first across a corn field and then up the alfalfa field to the tree stand.

After crossing the corn field I carefully crossed a thick hedgerow about twenty yards wide. When I got to the edge I carefully eased forward and scanned each direction for a possible feeding deer on the alfalfa. "All clear, darn, I thought." I had my "smoke pole" capped so if I had to shoot, all I needed to do is cock the hammer back and pull the trigger.

Slowly and quietly I walked up to the top of the field in the direction of the tree stand. Then where the field has a road to it I could see deep into the north end of the alfalfa field and I spotted a lone deer browsing with its head down. Good thing too, if it spotted me it would have spooked and in a bound or two it would have been in the woods and long gone ....

Carefully, I slowly dropped to one knee then flat on my belly. Some deep breathing while I thought of a stalk plan was needed to help calm me down. The best thing would be for me to belly crawl up the hill and then belly crawl down some to where I could see the deer. Then I could take a deadly accurate laying down shot on the deer's vital shoulder, lung or neck area. I thanked the Lord for my having both buck and doe tags because I could not tell if it was a spike horn or a doe.

My belly crawl stalk took fifteen or twenty minutes, I guess. Since I had never done this maneuver I was very careful. Finally, I could just raise my head and see through the alfalfa that the deer was still there feeding. It was like it was there waiting for me. When I could finally get my muzzleloader aiming in front of me through the alfalfa it was time to aim and fire a fatal round ball.

Now I am very confident in my rifle. If I did miss the deer it would be my fault alone. Carefully I took aim at the deer's front shoulder area and it did not appear to have horns but it really did not matter. After a few relaxing breaths I took careful aim, held the rifle firm against my shoulder firmly and fired. First the smoke and then the KA-BOOM sound only a muzzleloader can make. Through the smoke I saw the deer jump into the air and then it vanished.

First I was mad that I had missed. Why did the deer not just fall over? Could I have missed? After calming down I reloaded the rifle with another round ball and paced off in the direction of my deer; it was 65 paces. When I reached the back of the field where the deer should be I could not find a blood trail, much less see a deer. Then I walked ten to fifteen paces through brush toward the woods and there was my doe. Yah, it was hit right where I was aiming, behind the shoulder, so it was a clean one shot kill.

I praised the Lord for the forty plus pounds of venison that deer would provide our family. It really was a beautiful day that was capped off by a successful hunt. Thank you Lord for the nutritious venison from this whitetail for my family.

A NOVEMBER I REMEMBER

Unfortunately the poor health that I was plagued with last deer season persisted on and off over this year also. With the New York shotgun deer season only six weeks away, I was seeing my doctor regularly so I could work and hopefully feel well enough to enjoy my traditional deer hunting vacation.

If you want to be selected in the New York lottery drawing for an additional doe tag you must buy your buck tag in August and then apply for a doe tag. So, after buying my buck tag I applied for my out-of-state doe tag. Now months later when it arrived in the mail I immediately started thinking about doing all the little things surrounding my expected deer hunt those few days before Thanksgiving. Now poor health or not, with planning there had to be a way that I could hunt enough on the Arliss farm in New York to take a buck or doe. I could not gamble on taking a Pennsylvania deer close to home since I still had not located a quality deer hunting location.

Again this season I was making the traditional deer hunting trip from Philadelphia, Pennsylvania to Mom and Dad's in Clyde, New York alone. Because of my wife, Gale's appreciation for tasty nutritious venison she encouraged me to deer hunt and that was all I needed to "just go out and do it." With my having both buck and doe deer tags I was going to try to take a deer as soon as possible and I promised to be home by noon on Thanksgiving Day at the latest. Gale and our daughter, Kelly, would have our holiday meal ready for us when I returned.

Our family went to Saturday evening mass and then we enjoyed a delicious crock pot meal with garlic bread and Burgundy wine called New Orleans Style Venison Gumbo. Yes, the recipe is one in this cookbook. A great venison meal like this is meant to psyche me up for the rigors of the deer hunt that might lie ahead of me.

After breakfast Sunday morning I packed my hunting gear for all kinds of weather because upstate New York weather is very unpredictable and drove to my Mom and Dad's home. Dad said, as usual, the friends at our restaurant were asking about me; if I was coming home this year to deer hunt again? Dad told them I was and promised I would be around the restaurant some for sure to see them and swap deer tales, too . . . .

Sunday evening I went to see our friends, Rog and Polly Arliss, who were the best man and matron of honor at our wedding; to visit and get the latest on deer hunting hot spots on their farm. Roger's Mom and Dad, Bill and Ella, were at home, too, so I stopped to visit and have coffee with them. They are nice people. Rog and his brother, Larry and I grew up hunting, fishing and even went to high school and played sports together. Rog and Larry are known to be two of the hardest farm workers in all of New York State as far as I know. But they manage to make time to deer hunt and spend time socializing with our hunting crew every deer season.

At Rog's home we talked about anything and everything for a couple of hours but I was most concerned to learn that they were not seeing the number of deer they had been seeing in years past. There were a variety of reasons for the continuing decline in the deer population according to Rog but the biggest one was the effect of the increased number of doe tags having been issued in the hunting zone over the last three deer seasons.

Around 5 A.M. on this Monday opener I was woken up by my Dad, as usual. He was getting an earlier than usual start to get all those hungry deer hunters a hearty breakfast at Loder's Restaurant, Savannah, New York before they challenged the whitetail deer. Over the years most of the deer hunters in our Finger Lakes area do not take trophy buck. However, the deer eat well because of all the corn and alfalfa available to them since it is primarily dairy farming country. It is the exception not the rule that our area hunters do not prize the venison they take from a whitetail deer be it from a buck or doe for that matter.

Sick or not I was one of the earliest deer hunters of our crew to arrive at the Arliss farm. I was not sleeping well at the time and the enthusiasm for that first deer hunt in a year did not help me sleep, either. Bill Arliss asked if I brought my family up with me and I explained that I would only hunt these first three days before heading back to Philadelphia for our own family Thanksgiving with Gale and Kelly.

Rog and Larry Arliss soon arrived. They said with many of the local farms being sold to a prosperous developer to build a large game refuge they had not been seeing the sizable deer herd the farm had when they had deer crop damage years ago. They had not heard from many of the hunting crew from our old , once large, hunting party about wanting to deer hunt this season, either. Without enough hunters to have organized deer drives, my good fortune to take a whitetail of either sex in only three days then would be dependent solely on me to skillfully take one with my shotgun or muzzleloader from a deer stand, regardless of the weather.

If I recall it was only Rog, Larry, and I that deer hunted that opening morning. With the temperature around 30 degrees and the wind just "howling" it was not the time for a fair weather deer hunter. From daylight on, the sound of shotgun fire was noticeably reduced and to my surprise none of our old hunting crew showed up later in the day. No deer were seen that morning, however. I was forced to still and stand hunt in three different locations on the farm that day.

At about 2:30 P.M. I decided to climb into a sturdy looking tree stand that was at the end of a hedgerow that divided two corn fields behind Roger's house. With my scoped 12 ga. Ithaca deer slayer shotgun I could take a long shot on either sex deer if a fatal shot presented itself.

After an hour and half of carefully scanning two different corn fields I spotted one, two, three, four doe crossing the corn field to my left, but the whole three to four minutes they were in view they were too far or moving too fast for my shotgun shooting skill. I could only hope that soon a buck would show up trailing the doe and that he may mistakenly take a different line crossing the corn field and thus giving me a good fatal shot.

Our Lord was thinking of me because fifteen minutes after the doe had crossed, a lone deer was now cautiously making its way across the corn field to my right. With the high winds and darkness approaching this deer was very cautiously moving in my direction but it did not have a rack. When the deer was in shooting range I set my shotgun on the rail of the tree stand and scoped it. Then I could see it was a spike buck and not very big at all. It continued walking toward the hedgerow but now it was angling away from me, and I had to decide whether to take the deer or let it pass. Some voice said it is only opening day so what is your hurry. Wait and see if you can take a big deer, especially one with big horns. I passed it up.

For the next fifteen to twenty minutes I thought this decision over and while it was logical I may have made a costly mistake. Without our hunting party there to help move the deer in deer drives, there was a chance that over the next two days I would not get an opportunity to shoot another deer, period. Then my family and I would go a year without venison and it cost me about $180 in licenses and expenses to make this hunt, besides. Ah, now where is that spike buck again?

My hunter's diary reads — "When I saw movement along the hedgerow I was perched in and it was a deer, I felt a blessing from God." It was the spike buck walking up the other side of my hedgerow and walking right toward me. On this second chance if I got a good shot I would take the deer.

I rested my shotgun on the tree stand rail, eased off the safety and waited for the buck. At about 30 yards I squeezed off a slug at the deer's front shoulder. The shot was fatal so I climbed down from the stand and field dressed it just before dark. Wow, was I happy .... That is the good news, as they say. The bad news, though, after I got the deer to the dirt road near my car, I could not find my car keys. Somehow I had lost them from my pocket during the day's hunt. A bitter-sweet feeling came over me. With the problems caused by losing the car keys I did not feel so happy about having just taken my spike buck. It was a long, dark, cold walk up the dirt road to the Arliss farm.

Larry drove me back in his truck to get the tagged deer and then he drove me to my Mom and Dad's home in Clyde. Then I called my wife to first tell her the good news about getting my buck. Embarrassed, I explained about somehow losing my car keys and I would need her to send me one as soon as possible.

I borrowed my sister's car to hunt for a doe the next two days while I was waiting for my car keys to arrive. But I never fired a shot because there weren't any deer anywhere. To this day I feel it was our Lord's blessing to send that spike buck back to me for a *second chance shot*. After my hand processing the deer over Thanksgiving week-end we got about forty pounds of great venison. Thank you, Lord, for the venison from my buck ....

THE GIFT

For several years Jim Fowler and I have been friends. We at times were brought together because we both worked for the same company. We also had to swap our hunting or fishing tales anytime we talked. In 1994 I was promoted to an Account Manager job in Pittsburgh, Pennsylvania. When Jim heard about the move he called one day to invite me to hunt whitetails with him and his nephew, Mark Wiltshire, just south of Steubenville, Ohio, come shot gun deer season.

It is a tradition for Jim and his wife, Carol, to drive up to Steubenville the week of Thanksgiving to vacation with their family. The fourteen hour drive from Macon, Georgia is not a problem for Jim because he knows he will enjoy three or four days of fine deer hunting before he returns to Macon. Just the season before Mark had taken a fine 10 point buck. When Jim said doe tags were available and doe could be taken, often easily, if I did not score on a big buck. I agreed to pay for the expensive out of state Ohio big game license and join him and Mark.

We talked a few times before the deer season. Jim sent me a map and said it is just over an hour's drive to Mary's, his sister's house, where he would be staying. Jim called the evening before the Monday opener because it had been raining off and on for the past two days and more was coming. He still did not have to talk me into going, however. I told him I would be there at six A.M. sharp, rain gear and all. Then it rained *all* night long!

At 4 A.M. I was up and by 4:30 A.M. I was driving south at sixty-five MPH. Rain or no rain it was finally the opening day of deer season and it was possible my date with a trophy buck lay ahead; and as if I needed a better reason to hunt, we were out of venison again. Funny how every year that happens. We manage to stretch our venison meals out to last most of the year making sure to have freezer space for fresh venison by first Monday after Thanksgiving. This year was no different. I used one of my last venison roasts to make a huge red beans and rice dish that we would all be having at Mary and Glen's house on our lunch break opening day. Over the years I have always enjoyed cooking venison and sharing it with family, friends and other hunting partners I happened to hook up with. The proof is in the writing of this venison cookbook.

I arrived on time and met Jim and Mark at Mary and Glen's home. We were all eager to get into the woods to stake out our deer stands, so with flashlights in hand we were soon off into the darkness, rain and all. The rain was not as hard to take as the warm, howling winds. Mark walked me to a ground blind location, said to come back down the ridge to his mom's around noon for a dish of that venison red beans & rice if I did not take a deer before that. He wished me luck and walked off to his favorite buck scrape line.

When daylight came I could sneak around a bit to look for fresh deer sign and to select a shooting area based on the deer trails and sign around. I was confident of my hunting spot so I used my tree seat to sit motionless all morning. The rain let up by noon but the wind was gusting all morning. Limbs were falling around me every few minutes and I was glad I was not in a deer stand even on this opening day. All morning I was wishing and praying to get a shot at a whitetail. I called "here deer" to myself over and over again; even asking the Lord for his help in taking a whitetail for its prized venison.

At 8:30 and 10 A.M. I heard shotguns firing several times in Mark and Jim's direction so despite my not even seeing a deer I was hopeful that they had been able to "put some venison in the freezer" and maybe share a little with me if I do not get my own deer, as hunters often do. At lunch I learned both Mark and Jim had filled their doe tags so this afternoon they would be hunting for bucks only. Although the weather improved none of us even saw a deer the rest of the afternoon. After a long day's hunt, at dark I told Mark and Jim I would go home, get some much needed rest and be back at 6 A.M. to hunt with them.

The second day of the 1994 Ohio deer season dawned sunny and mild, since the storm blew through. For an hour or more after daylight I was entertained by who knows how many wild turkeys. What a sight. They were flying overhead, landing in the tops of nearby trees, and walking all around me. It was a beautiful morning to be in the woods, despite the steep, hard climb that got me up on this ridge.

After hours on watch for the opportunity to take my either sex deer during this Ohio deer season, and after 26 years of deer hunting I was blessed with perhaps a once in a life time chance to take my first trophy whitetail buck. At mid morning from my ridge top perch I luckily spotted a buck 60+ yards below me and swiftly moving down the mountain. Automatically I left my tree seat and rested my 12 gauge, scope sighted Ithaca Deerslayer against the tree I was sitting on and as I looked to find the buck in my scope, I found it loping down the brush covered mountain 70+ yards away.

Nervously, I pushed the safety off and squeezed off a first slug at the back of the running BUCK. I missed and pumped another slug into the shotgun. When I looked through the scope to attempt a second shot I found the buck in the brush. It had stopped after hearing the first shot and was deciding where to run.

THANK GOD I was blessed with that second shot opportunity because my relaxed second slug hit the buck in the vitals and it went down for good.

It was over 210 lbs. live weight, and was a 3 year old deer. It had a distinctively high and long tined 9 point rack. After 25 years of whitetail deer hunting I finally took my mountable buck. Ah, I had just the wall space picked out.

*Also very important: Lots of delicious venison for our family, too.

THANK YOU LORD

A beautiful picture of this buck mount can be seen on the back cover of our first venison cookbook.

THE SIX POINT THAT DID NOT GET AWAY

No problem with my waking up at four A.M. because it was opening day of the fall wild turkey season in Ohio. Mark Wiltshire, my hunting partner, and I had worked several gobblers with our calls earlier in the spring but we were not successful. This was my chance, because I had a better knowledge of the woods, and I could bag a turkey of either sex. Mark, on the other hand, would be bow hunting for deer, either sex.

After a seventy mile drive, I arrived at Mark's home and by six A.M. we were using flash lights to guide us up the brush clogged ridge behind his home. Before splitting up, my flashlight was used to help Mark light his smoke pole buck attractant. The plan was for me to leave Mark in his deer tree stand and hunt turkey on the ridge above and away from him. After lunch I would work my way back down the ridge, occasionally stopping to set up to call turkey. This way, if my scent or turkey calling spooked any deer, there would be a chance they could pass within Mark's bow shooting range.

It was a beautiful fall morning to be way up on this ridge when the sun came up. Only two times all morning did I have turkeys answering my call, but I did not get sight of any turkeys either time. About nine A.M. I spotted a lone doe silently walking down the ridge toward me. When she saw me she stopped to stare thirty seconds or so and then turned to back track to safety. A deer will usually do this back track maneuver if they are leery about forward safe travel. A deer thinks because it was safe traveling to this point, it is safe to travel back some and then adjust their travel if necessary.

About ten thirty A.M. I was sitting on a log and calling turkeys occasionally. The woods were sunny and quiet, so when a
deer snorted from ten yards behind me I nearly fell off the log, dropping my gun, too. A deer will snort like that, with their nose that is
fifty times more sensitive than a human, when it smells something
it does not like. After recovering my senses, I turned to see two doe
bounding further up the ridge above me. It gets really thick with
briars up there. That is why I was hunting the ledge below them.

Then, after finishing a noon time sandwich, as planned, I was
to slowly hunt my way down the ridge to Mark. I positioned myself
on the wood line below the briars behind me. I was silently moving
and occasionally sitting to call turkeys, but the turkeys never did
answer my call. Time was running out because my last set up was
one hundred and fifty yards from where Mark was in his tree. Before I could sit down after attaching my tree seat, I heard another
loud deer snort up in the briars behind me. Although I could not
see the deer bound away, there could have been two or more, judg-
ing from the racket they made cutting through the thick briars.

Since we had only an hour more to hunt, I decided to take a
fox squirrel or two if given the opportunity. As luck would have it,
I did not have to wait long for big Mr. Fox Squirrel. He was moving
fast to a destination unknown to me, but I managed to bag him on
my second shot. Thirty minutes later I picked up my "trophy" squirrel and slowly worked my way down toward Mark.

When I say slowly worked my way down to Mark, I mean it.
This ridge is very steep and slippery, especially walking on the muddy
deer runs. Walking carefully down a deer run I noticed a deer
crumpled below me. Suddenly I slid down the bank with gun and
the squirrel going in different directions. My head hit a tree and I
was smacked starry eyed before I hit the ground. It was several
minutes before I managed to get to my knees and yes sir the deer
was still there and it was a buck.

I yelled for Mark that I had his deer up here. He answered
saying he was headed up my way. When he arrived he said he lost
sight of the six point after he shot at it and was looking for it down
the ridge. I congratulated Mark and said "it's a good thing I came
down from above" or we may not have found it. "Oh, Mark, when
did you shoot this buck?" His reply was "an hour ago." "Before I
shot the squirrel, then?" "Ya, right."

"Well, that was when I set up the last time one hundred and
fifty yards above you. I heard a deer snort and then heard deer running through the briars behind me. I must have spooked them and
we were blessed this time because they ran to you within bow range,

even. Way to go Mark, with your good shooting you did not let me down."

Mark did the field dressing honors and together we got the buck down the ridge to where we could get at it with his truck. It goes to show, some deer hunting plans can and do work out. Let us not forget to give thanks to our Lord for the venison from this nice buck, Mark.

MAKING A CASE FOR BONING OUT YOUR DEER

Now you have already read the good deer tale about Mark skill fully putting the fatal arrow into the six point buck that was spooked by my scent. Here is the rest of the story.

Over the past six months or so I had talked with Mark regularly about ideas I had to include while writing our first venison cookbook. The "Boning Out Your Deer" article was extremely important to include because it had proven to me and would to other deer hunters that processing your deer yourself can mean better tasting venison for your family's dinner table. It is *your* quality control of the process that makes a difference.

When we got Mark's buck back to his house he politely asked me if I would not mind boning out his buck. I knew the amount of work involved in it, but to prove my venison quality improvement point to his family, who was not too fond of the venison they get back from their butcher, I agreed to hand process it for him.

Once home, just as I have always done many, many times over the years, I quartered the buck, carefully removed the fillets and the back straps and put them in two of my ice filled quality coolers. I watched the ice and turned the venison occasionally over the next 2 days. On the third day it was time to actually bone out the front shoulder meat and hind quarters.

The shoulder meat was put into a Dutch oven and weighed. Later I thought to separate three pounds because Mark and his wife love to make venison jerky for them and their two young boys. The rest of the venison shoulder I ground and mixed an equal amount of hamburger to it to make lean, great tasting venisonburger for them.

Each of the other two hind quarters were deboned as in the article in our first cookbook, "Boning Out Your Deer." The hocks and shanks were saved for stew meat in all kinds of recipes. Each hind quarter was saved as is in a Dutch oven for a final butchering according to Mark's preferred package size of steaks and roasts. The fillets and tenderloins were saved separately. All the venison was then stored in our refrigerator until the next day when Mark and I would do the final cut, wrapping, and freezing of his buck.

Oh, I forgot to mention, when you process a deer there are always venison trimmings that come from the neck area, ribs, front shoulders, etc. that should be saved for stew or jerky. Since their jerky venison was already saved from shoulder venison, I used the saved trimmings to make a recipe called "Marks' Buck In A Bag" and baked it so we could share a great meal after we were finished putting Mark and his wife, Cindy's venison in their freezer. What a great idea that turned out to be.

Mark and I were still cutting and wrapping his venison when Cindy came home. She was quick to ask if we saved any venison for jerky. I remember I told her, yes, there is a three pound bag in your refrigerator. She looked at and smelled the venison. She commented it did not look nor smell like venison they get back from their butcher. Well, I have carefully deboned it and removed all fat and tallow from the venison as I do for myself and you are going to really like eating this venison. In fact you will see a deer's venison represents thirty to sixty pounds of nutritiously delicious meals for your family. It is just not "jerky meat." To show you what I mean, Cindy, I have prepared a venison roast called "Mark's Buck In A Bag" and it is heating up in your oven now. Here is the recipe. When we are done wrapping venison we will sample the roast so you can see how good this venison will taste.

It is easy to remember how much we all enjoyed eating that venison roast together. It was a special meal that will not be forgotten for a long time, if ever.

Oh, the next time I talked to Mark I asked how they liked the venison. He said it was all great, but now Cindy was mad at him. She asked to make a venisonburger meat loaf and he would not let her. He felt it best to save that great venisonburger for pasta sauce and chili, not for meat loaf. I just commented, Mark, it is OK. Venisonburger makes great meat loaf, too. In this case it will also bring peace in the family.

Whatever happened to the three pounds of venison that was left for venison jerky? That "Mark's Buck In A Bag" venison roast was so tasty they did not make the jerky but instead used it to make the "Buck In A Bag" recipe several days later, for a second time.

Hand processed, quality cared for venison, like discussed earlier in our first cookbook, *Quality Venison, Homemade Recipes & Homespun Deer Tales*, does make a real difference to the venison you can prepare for your family and friends, so give it a try!

ANOTHER BIG ONE GOT AWAY

This year, as usual, the Monday after Thanksgiving was the open ing of the gun deer season in Ohio. As I was gathering my shotgun and other hunting gear around supper time, the phone rang. My wife, Gale, answered it and found out it was Jim Fowler, a hunting partner of mine who had come up to visit his relatives and hunt deer again this season. It was good to know Jim was in town OK and he, his nephew, Mark, and I would be deer hunting together again in the morning for the fourth year now.

Like most deer hunters, my getting up at four A.M. was not a problem because of the excitement and anticipation that always comes with being at my choice spot before daylight on opening day of gun deer season. After meeting Mark and Jim we decided where our morning watch stands would be and we split up, carrying flashlights to get each of us where we wanted to be by legal shooting time.

Carefully I climbed a ridge over-looking the woods below where Mark and Jim would hunt. We all had either sex deer tags, so our chances of getting venison for our families was fairly good if our shotgun slug shooting was accurate. There was the usual amount of gun fire that morning, but at about nine-thirty A.M. shots below indicated Mark or Jim had likely taken a deer.

By noon I had seen only two doe. I did not have a shot because it was after they smelled my human scent. I was disappointed. Back at the house for lunch I learned Jim did fill his doe tag around nine-thirty as I had expected. Mark saw deer but did not get a shot. After our hearty lunch of my venison chili, we headed back out for our afternoon watch. After talking with our resident guide (Mark) I decided on a new ground watch location. Deer sign was everywhere. About half way up the ridge there were two parallel deer trails, so I hitched my tree seat between them where I could see fairly well. The location was typical of deer woods, you know, dense in places and lots of small trees. It would have been great to be up in a tree stand. (Hey, you should have thought about that earlier, big white hunter). Maybe for next year!

The temperature was comfortable and the woods were quiet because of the rain the day before. As customary, I was slowly scanning woods as far as I could see all around me for deer. Ask any deer hunter if it is not uncanny how an animal as large as a deer can suddenly appear and be staring at you from thirty yards away. You think how did it get there? Deer most always spot the hunter before you can spot them, even when the hunter is not moving and the deer is. That is exactly what happened to this "experienced" deer hunter.

When I spotted this huge doe at 35-40 yards it was stopped and staring at me. It had, of course, caught me by surprise. After calming down, I slowly eased behind a tree to raise my shotgun. Carefully I shifted my weight from behind the tree while aiming at the doe. It had not moved and was still staring at me. There wasn't another deer near her that I could see, so I fired with hopes of filling my doe tag with legal and nutritious venison for our freezer.

When the shotgun fired, the doe bolted as if it were hit. Unfortunately, out of the corner of my right eye, I saw another deer bolt away. It was not 20 yards behind the doe but concealed by some brush. It was a big deer, too, only this one had *big horns.* This buck had apparently stopped far enough behind the sentry doe that I may not have been able to see the buck in the brush even if I studied the brush behind the doe more carefully before shooting. So, I may still have made the decision to shoot after patiently looking some distance behind her only to have the buck bound away untouched after shooting at the doe. Then again, had I waited a few minutes I may have been able to see the buck standing or moving slowly through the brush and I would have had a rare opportunity to take a nice trophy buck.

I learned my lesson to always patiently look behind a sentry or mature lone doe expecting to see a buck trailing her. The buck may be twenty yards or twenty minutes behind her especially if the rut is on.

Sure hope that was not the only chance I will have to take a deer for our freezer. A year without venison to enjoy — is a real disappointment especially after I made a mistake ... Oh! By the way, I missed the big doe. And that's a big disappointment. My wife will have something disappointing to say about this deer hunt. As if I do not feel bad enough already?

COOKING MORE HOMEMADE VENISON RECIPES IN STEVE AND GALE'S COUNTRY KITCHEN

"Ah, even I must admit that new venison recipe smells awfully good!"

PREFACE

You have had a great day in the field and it does not matter what day of the deer season it is because you just harvested your deer. You are happy and feel the satisfaction that comes with knowing you have fresh venison for your family for next year. I, for one, strongly feel this way.

Some of us hunters are fortunate enough to be married to a special kind of woman who enjoys cooking the venison we bring home, as mine does. Some men are like myself and enjoy hunting and cooking venison creatively and traditionally year after year. But many men, especially young hunters do not know enough about venison's nutritious value, and the satisfaction and enjoyment that comes from eating the venison you harvest, process and then cook for yourself and others year in and year out. With deer hunting success they will learn to appreciate their venison, not only at deer camp but on their family's dinner table, too.

The collection of these 150 proven recipes here-in comes together after over thirty years of venison and wild game cooking of all kinds. We are confident you will appreciate the very consistent recipe quality for yourself. Here is to good hunting and better quality venison meals for you and your family and friends.

DISPELLING THE MYTH OF GAMY VENISON

The objective of our efforts in the writing of our first venison cookbook titled, *Quality Venison: Homemade Recipes and Homespun Deer Tales,* was to share our knowledge and that of knowledgeable others, so that all deer hunters could have the invaluable "How To Guide" for "Quality Venison" from field to freezer. By following the information in this guide and hand processing their own deer they can be assured their venison will never be "gamy". They can then confidently enjoy cooking nutritious venison in any of our recipes for their family and friends.

STEVE AND THE OUTDOORS,
THE WORDS ARE INTERCHANGEABLE

As a youngster growing up in the Finger Lakes region of upstate New York, Steve was a cub scout and boy scout who from a young age loved camping, fishing, and later hunting. Inclement weather did not stop him—he'd just do it!

At the early age of twelve he started hunting small game and later hunted deer and waterfowl, too. That waterfowl excitement got to him at an early age, and he became an avid waterfowl hunter as well as deer hunter wherever corporate America has taken us since. Steve has been a National Rifle Association member as long as I have known him; after all these years he still is a Ducks Unlimited member and usually a fund raising committee member. He is also a part-time volunteer for western Pennsylvania in the Hunters Share the Harvest Program. This program informs hunters how they can share their blessing of venison from the whitetail deer with the less fortunate through venison donations to area food banks, the Salvation Army, etc. He says it helps him feel he is giving something back from his love of the outdoors. You know . . . . I like that, and our Lord does too . . .

—*Gale Loder*

MEMORIES

Memories, no one can take memories from you. You can lose a job, run out of money, lose a friend or loved one, but memories are here forever. And one of my fondest memories since Steve and I married twenty-two years ago has to do with Steve deer hunting for venison. We had been married for a mere three years, give or take a few months. We moved to Roanoke, Virginia from Binghamton, New York so Steve could hopefully further his career. The new job did not work out, so test number one for our family began.

We hadn't been married long enough to have saved much money for a rainy day. Fortunately God was watching over us. With God's guidance and the help of family and friends we made it through our first crisis. Steve hunted for venison when he wasn't hunting for a job. After going out several times and not seeing anything he finally came home with *that deer!* He tried to surprise me but I had been anxiously awaiting his return and saw him when he drove in the driveway. I saw the trunk of the car was open so I ran outside and nearly flew through the driver's window of the car in excitement. We would have tasty, nutritious meals though the winter and into the spring after all. I was so thankful for the venison that I even helped him package the venison once it was processed.

—*Gale Loder*

WHERE'S THE BEEF?

And then there was the time we were *out of venison* and Labor Day week-end was approaching. With nice weather we planned a picnic. Steve usually smokes a chicken or pork roast along with a venison roast, but no venison was to be found in our freezer . . . After Steve returned from the grocery store I was curious as to what kinds of meat we would be sharing with our neighbors, so I had to check the refrigerator. Venison is our BEEF, so I was unpleasantly surprised when next to the large roasting chicken was a beef roast. A big beef roast, too. I already knew I was not eating it. Venison has me spoiled!

To voice my displeasure I had to find Steve in the garage. When I did, I remember looking him straight in the eyes and yelled "BEEF - BEEF" and awaited a response. His only excuse was it was to be tested in a new venison recipe that would be written in our *Quality Venison* cookbook. He figured if the recipe made a beef roast taste good, using quality venison would make it even better. He was right, the recipe is "Company's Coming Venison Roast" page 62 in our first *Quality Venison* cookbook.

—*Gale Loder*

A Few Words About Cooking Venison

By Bob Mitchell, Editor, Pennsylvania Game News Magazine

When I shot my first deer, back in 1979, just getting the deer was the culmination of the hunt. I took it to a processor, who did a good job of boning everything out, but from that point on I was pretty much lost when it came to actually cooking the meat.

Since then, however, I've been extremely lucky when it comes to getting deer, and killing the animal is no longer the end of the hunting experience, it's more like the beginning. I've learned how to dress and care for the animal, I'm careful about aging the meat, and I now do my own butchering. My goal each deer season is not to kill a deer. My goal is to get a supply of top quality venison that I can use to make mouth-watering meals throughout the year. For me, the hunting experience ends not in the field, but on the table, and one of the most enjoyable aspects of deer hunting has become trying new recipes.

Venison Cooking Tips

1.   FRESH HERBS — will improve a recipe's flavor — generally not practical — try this occasionally for a special meal.

2.   RECIPES — can substitute other vegetables and similar amounts of spices, too.   Recipes seldom say it, but if needed thin a stew or pasta sauce with water for desired consistency.

3.   God forbid any of us are out of delicious venison to prepare, but you can use our recipes substituting similar amounts of ground beef, pork sausage, beef steak or roast for venison.

4.   VENISON RIBS — Who cooks them? Bake at 400 degrees for 20 minutes — turn — bake 10 minutes. This gets rid of most of the fat. Add 2 pounds to crock pot and add onion, garlic, barbecue sauce and water to cover. Bake on high for 5-6 hours, adding more water if necessary. Delicious for sure. . . .

A WHITETAIL'S VENISON

Venison is very nutritious and good for you, too. I have heard of doctors telling patients the only meat they can eat was venison. Consider the following. A comparison was made between a 3.5 oz. portion of venison and other meat and salmon:

- Venison has ¼ the fat of lean roast beef.

- Venison has ½ the fat of lean ham or salmon.

- Venison has ⅕ the saturated fat of lean roast beef.

- Venison is lower in saturated fat than lean ham or salmon.

- Venison per portion has less calories than lean ham, salmon, or a skinless chicken breast.

- Venison per portion has 40% less calories.

- Venison per portion has 10-15% more protein than lean roast beef, lean ham, and salmon and the same amount of protein as a lean skinless chicken breast.

So, whether you process your own deer or let a processor you trust to do it right, when your venison has been carefully aged (DO NOT LET THE FAT SPOIL BECAUSE IT IS GAMY) all fat, bone and tallow removed during processing, and then double wrapped for freezing, you will always have deliciously nutritious venison dishes.

—Jim Zumbo & Steve Loder

COOKING VENISON SOUTHERN STYLE

*T*his collection of recipes was prepared over the years we lived, worked, and hunted the whitetail deer in the southern states of Virginia, Tennessee, and Mississippi.

People in the south love beef and pork barbecue, collard greens, black eyed peas, okra; and cayenne pepper or hot sauce is the spice of life. They also prefer the all-in-one or casserole dishes that can be used or frozen for a future tasty meal.

Southerner's are proud of their tradition as hunters and fishermen who yearly provide nutritious game and fish for their family's dinner table. In thousands of families venison is a nutritious staple to their family budget. Their recipes are also often easy and fun to prepare. We encourage you, as always, to substitute ingredients, change vegetables, or change spice amounts to suit your taste. Cooking venison, like anything else, should be fun and not "rocket science." We trust you will enjoy trying these southern style favorite recipes as much as we have.

*T*his recipe is "hot Cajun" style jambalaya so you may want to cut back on black and cayenne pepper some and add more to individual servings if preferred. A tasty southern stew indeed .....

VENISON-SAUSAGE JAMBALAYA

2½ tablespoons butter

6 hot sausage links (about 1 pound), cut into small pieces (if using leftovers, add 5 to 10 minutes before serving so they are heated)

1½ pounds venison roast, cubed

1 large onion, chopped

2 small green bell peppers, chopped

2 ribs celery, chopped (1 cup)

Spice mix (recipe follows)

1½ teaspoons minced garlic

2 cups uncooked rice

8-10 oz. frozen okra

2½ to 3 cups beef broth

Water - (optional)

Add butter to large saucepan over medium heat. Add sausage and cook until lightly browned, about 8 minutes. Add cubed venison and cook until lightly browned, about 6 to 8 minutes. Stir constantly. Add chopped vegetables. After 3 to 4 minutes, add spice mix and garlic. Stir, scraping the bottom of the pan. Add rice, okra, and beef broth. Cook, stirring uncovered, until stock is absorbed and rice is tender. Add water if necessary. Remove bay leaves. Makes 4 servings. Enjoy!

SPICE MIX: Combine 2 bay leaves, 1½ teaspoons salt, ¾ teaspoon cayenne pepper, 1 teaspoon black pepper, ¾ teaspoon chili powder, 1 teaspoon dried thyme, and 1 teaspoon parsley.

STOVE TOP SAUSAGE-NOODLE CREOLE

1 pound venison sausage
1 medium onion, sliced
2 cloves garlic, diced
1 cup green pepper, diced
1 cup water
2 tablespoons salt
1/4 teaspoon black pepper

2 tablespoons Worcestershire sauce
2 (1 pound 3 oz.) cans stewed tomatoes
dash hot sauce - to taste
1/2 pound medium egg noodles

Cook sausage in skillet or Dutch oven over medium heat, turning often, until brown, about 10 minutes; remove. Sauté onion, garlic, and green pepper in 2 tablespoons butter until tender; add remaining ingredients and blend well. Return sausage to skillet and bring mixture to a boil. Lower temperature. Simmer, covered, stirring occasionally for 15 to 18 minutes or until noodles are tender.

MEXICAN VENISON CASSEROLE

1 pound venisonburger
1/3 cup onion, diced
2 cloves garlic, diced
1 can Rotel tomatoes, chopped
dash pepper sauce or cayenne pepper

salt and black pepper to taste
1 can cream of onion soup
1 pound nacho cheese chips
1 pound grated cheddar or colby cheese
1/2 cup bread crumbs

Mix venisonburger, onion and garlic. Cook in skillet until browned. Mix tomatoes, pepper sauce, salt, pepper, and onion soup together; set aside. In large casserole dish, layer as follows: half of burger mixture, half of nacho cheese chips; half of grated cheese; one-third of soup mixture. Repeat with remaining ingredients, layered as above. Top with bread crumbs. Bake in oven at 350 degrees for 15-20 minutes. A tasty treat.

DON'S EASY MEAT LOAF

2 pounds ground
  venisonburger
1½ cups fresh bread crumbs
1 cup warm water
½ teaspoon garlic powder
2 eggs, beaten

¾ cup catsup or salsa
1 pkg. onion soup mix
1 teaspoon chili powder
2 strips bacon, uncooked
1 (8 oz.) can tomato sauce

Mix all ingredients, except for bacon and tomato sauce. Place in loaf pan; cover with bacon and tomato sauce. Bake at 350 degrees for 1 hour.

This is a recipe from Sue, J.D.'s wife. J.D. is who I was deer hunting with in Mississippi after which I wrote the deer tale "A Case of Southern Hospitality." Our family found this easy dish simply delicious and you will too.

J.D.'s MEXICAN VENISON LOIN CHOPS

1 large size oven cooking bag
2 tablespoons flour
1 cup your thick, chunky salsa
  or picante sauce
1 tablespoon lemon juice
1 teaspoon chili powder
1 teaspoon garlic, diced

½ bunch green onions,
  chopped
1 to 1¼ pound venison loin
  chops
1 (16 oz.) can kidney beans
2 medium bell peppers, color
  of your choice, cut in cubes
⅛ teaspoon cayenne pepper

Preheat your oven to 350 degrees and then shake flour in oven cooking bag. Place in 13 x 9 inch baking pan and add salsa or picante sauce, lemon juice, chili powder, garlic, and onions to oven bag. Toss the closed bag several times to blend seasonings. Put your venison chops in the bag and spoon in beans, bell peppers, and cayenne pepper around the venison chops; blend. Close bag with nylon tie and cut 6 holes in bag. Bake until venison is tender 40 to 45 minutes. Let meal cool five minutes after baking and serve with brown rice and fresh tomato/vegetable salad. As always, Enjoy! Ole!!

A QUICK MARDI GRAS VENISON CHILI

2 cups diced cooked venison, cubed

1 can (14½ oz.) stewed tomatoes

1 can (8 oz.) tomato sauce

1 medium onion, chopped

1 green pepper, chopped

1 tablespoon chili powder

½ teaspoon ground cumin (optional)

¼ teaspoon cayenne pepper

½ teaspoon black pepper

1 (15¼ oz.) can kidney beans, drained

In Dutch oven, combine venison, tomatoes, tomato sauce, onion, green pepper, chili powder, cumin and cayenne and black pepper; cover and simmer 30 minutes. Stir in beans and simmer, uncovered, 30 minutes more. Pass the corn bread, Mom.

HERBS CAN MAKE A TASTE DIFFERENCE

Venison by itself has a delicious, rich "red" meat flavor, but as with any meat, seasonings enhance that flavor. Store bought seasonings work, but home grown herbs are the best. During the summer months I grow thyme and oregano outside in pots on our deck. I usually have parsley and chives growing inside all year long. This year I added basil. Besides being great enhancers to venison dishes, herbs make lovely house plants.

I would grow all my herbs inside in a controlled atmosphere if I had the room and proper lighting for them. One of my dreams is to one day have a green house so I can grow vegetables and herbs inside all year round because there is nothing like fresh, home grown vegetables such as tomatoes and bell peppers and herbs to enhance the flavor of the already tasty venison meals.

—Gale Loder

I had the opportunity to enjoy this recipe on the weekend before the opening of the Mississippi duck season when Dick and I were at duck camp. I liked the dish and Dick said a mallard's two breasts could be substituted if you did not have venison. You will like this one, too!

DICK'S CAJUN VENISON CREOLE

1 pound venison steak, thinly sliced

¹/₃ cup soy sauce

1 cup green onions, chopped

1 cup celery, diced

2 garlic cloves, diced

2 tablespoons butter

1 (10 oz.) pkg. frozen okra or lima beans

1 pound fresh tomatoes, chopped or 1 (14¹/₂ oz.) can stewed tomatoes

1 cup water

Cut venison into 1 inch cubes; put in a small bowl. Add soy sauce and mix well; let it soak 15 to 30 minutes. In medium frying pan sauté onions, celery, and garlic in butter. Stir in okra or lima beans, tomatoes, and water. Bring to a boil. Reduce heat to simmer 15 minutes. Stir in venison and simmer 45 to 60 minutes or until tender. *Optional - Creole is mild Cajun cooking - You could add hot sauce or cayenne pepper to taste after serving. So good and so easy to prepare, too . . . . .

*Who said easy venison cooking can't be delicious and healthy, too! *For a spicier Creole taste add an extra 1/4 to 1/2 teaspoon chili powder or cayenne pepper to last 15 minutes of cooking time. So—tasty!*

EASY LOUISIANA VENISON CREOLE

1 pound venison steak, sliced very thin

1/2 cup green onions, chopped

1/2 cup green pepper, chopped

1/2 cup celery, chopped

2 tablespoons butter

1/4 cup sliced green or black olives

1 cup water

1/2 teaspoon black pepper

1 pkg. Lipton's Spanish Rice mix

1 (14 1/2 oz.) can stewed tomatoes

1/4 to 1/2 teaspoon chili powder or cayenne pepper (optional)

In a Dutch oven start by browning venison with onion, bell pepper and celery in butter, and set aside. Combine your remaining ingredients to your Dutch oven. Bring to a boil while stirring well. Cover and simmer until most liquid is absorbed (10-15 minutes). Add venison back to Dutch oven; cover and simmer 15 minutes or so to serve hot.

SUNNY SUNDAY CASSEROLE

1 1/2 cups instant rice, uncooked

1 can cream of mushroom soup

1 can cream of celery soup

2 pounds venisonburger or sausage

1 cup milk

2 cloves garlic, diced

1 envelope onion soup mix

Mix rice and creamed soups in 9 x13 inch casserole dish. In large frying pan brown venison. Add venison, milk, and garlic to casserole, stir and cover with envelope of onion soup mix. Cover dish with foil and bake in oven at 350 degrees for 1 hour. Add corn bread for a great meal.

A DUCK HUNTER'S VENISON DISH

1 pound ground
  venisonburger/sausage
1 teaspoon salt
dash each black and cayenne
  pepper
2 tablespoons butter
1/2 cup celery, sliced
1/2 cup onion, chopped

1/4 cup bell pepper, chopped
1 pkg. macaroni and cheese
  dinner
2 cups (1 pound can) whole
  tomatoes, chopped
1 (6 oz.) can tomato paste
2 cups frozen okra

Season venison with salt and black and cayenne pepper; and brown in butter in a large Dutch oven. Add celery, onion, and bell pepper; cook until tender. Prepare macaroni and cheese dinner as directed; add to venison with remaining ingredients and mix lightly. Simmer 15 to 30 minutes.

GREEN PEPPER VENISON STEAK

1 tablespoon soy sauce
2 cloves garlic, diced
1/4 cup olive oil
1 pound venison steak, cut
  into 1 inch cubes
1/2 teaspoon salt
1 medium onion, chopped
1/2 cup celery, diced

1 medium bell pepper,
  chopped
2 teaspoons cornstarch
1/4 cup water
2 ripe tomatoes, cut into
  eighths
1/2 can tomato soup
cooked rice or noodles

Mix soy sauce, garlic and olive oil; pour over cut up steak in large frying pan. Refrigerate and let stand 1 hour. Brown venison on all sides. Add salt, onion, celery and bell pepper. Cover and cook over low heat 5-10 minutes or until vegetables are tender. Stir in cornstarch dissolved in 1/4 cup water; stir until thickened. Add tomatoes and soup; cover and cook at least 45 minutes or until venison is tender. Serve over rice or noodles.

I was fortunate to hunt deer, waterfowl, and small game with Dan two seasons while living in Bristol, Tennessee. One evening our families gathered at his house where we really enjoyed this tasty pasta dish.

DAN'S EASY TENNESSEE PASTA

1½ pounds venisonburger or sausage

2 tablespoons butter

1 onion, diced finely (1 cup)

2 (16 oz.) cans Italian-style tomato sauce

1 teaspoon garlic salt

½ teaspoon oregano

black pepper to taste

1 (8 oz.) bag extra-broad egg noodles

8 oz. diary sour cream

4 oz. ricotta cheese

½ to 1 cup cheddar cheese, grated

Preheat oven to 350 degrees. Stir fry venisonburger or sausage in butter in a large frying pan over medium-high heat until tender. Add onion, tomato sauce, garlic salt, oregano, and black pepper. Turn heat down to low and simmer 20 minutes. While meat sauce simmers, cook noodles as directed on package; drain.

In a bowl mix thoroughly sour cream, ricotta cheese, and cooked noodles. In a 13 x 9 x 2 inch pan, spread a layer of meat sauce. Next, spread a thin layer of noodles. Continue to layer remaining meat sauce and noodle mixture. Sprinkle grated cheese on top. Place in preheated oven and bake for 10 minutes or until thoroughly heated and cheese melts.

COUNTRY STYLE VENISON WITH BEANS

2 slices bacon, diced

4 venison loin steaks (1 pound), sliced ¼ inch thick

1 medium onion, chopped

2 cloves garlic, minced

1 teaspoon crushed oregano

1 (14½ oz.) can stewed tomatoes, chopped

1 (16 oz.) frozen green lima beans, drained

1 (8 oz.) can kidney beans, drained

In a large skillet, over low heat, cook bacon until just crisp. Raise heat to medium; stir in venison, onion, garlic, and oregano. Stir fry for 5 minutes. Add remaining ingredients; bring to boil. Reduce heat and simmer, uncovered 30 minutes. Season to taste with salt and pepper and hot sauce, if desired. Pass the biscuits, please ...

LOUISIANA VENISON CREOLE AND RICE

Flour to coat venison

2 pounds venison, cubed

3 tablespoons butter

½ bunch green onions, chopped

½ green pepper, chopped

2 cloves garlic, mined

1 (28 oz.) can stewed tomatoes

⅓ cup soy sauce

¼ teaspoon cayenne pepper

1 (10 oz.) pkg. frozen broccoli or okra, thawed and drained

hot cooked rice for 4 to 5

Lightly flour venison pieces. Brown on all sides in hot butter in large skillet or Dutch oven over medium heat; remove. Add onion, green pepper and garlic to same skillet or Dutch oven and sauté 5 minutes. Stir in tomatoes, soy sauce, and cayenne; bring to a boil. Arrange venison pieces in sauce. Cover and simmer 5 minutes, turning pieces over once. Stir in okra or broccoli; cover and simmer 10 minutes longer, or until okra or broccoli is tender. Serve venison and sauce over hot rice. Salt and pepper to taste.

SOUTHERN STYLE VENISON & SALSA BURRITOS

1 pound venisonburger or
   sausage

1¹/₂ tablespoons chili powder

¹/₂ teaspoon ground cumin

¹/₂ teaspoon salt

¹/₄ teaspoon black pepper

1¹/₄ cups prepared chunky
   salsa

1 pkg. (10 oz.) frozen chopped
   okra or broccoli, thawed
   and well drained

1 cup shredded cheddar
   cheese

8 medium flour tortillas,
   warmed

In a large skillet, brown venison over medium heat 10 minutes or until no longer pink, stirring occasionally. Pour off drippings, if any. Season venison with chili powder, cumin, salt, and black pepper. Stir in salsa and okra or broccoli; heat, cooking the okra or broccoli 15 minutes or until tender. Remove from heat; stir in cheese. Heat tortillas according to package directions. Spoon ¹/₂ cup venison mixture in center of each tortilla. Fold bottom edge up over filling; fold sides to center, overlapping edges. Makes 8 burritos. Ole!

TENNESSEE VENISON STEAK DELUXE

2 tablespoons olive oil

4 tablespoons flour

2 pounds venison steak,
   1 inch thick, cut in serving
   pieces

1 (10³/₄ oz.) can golden
   mushroom soup

1 teaspoon each salt and
   black pepper

2 soup cans water

1 cup diced celery

¹/₂ cup diced onions

1 cup fresh mushrooms,
   sliced

Heat olive oil in skillet, press flour into venison, and brown well. Put in 1 can soup, cover and simmer for half an hour. Add salt and black pepper. Pour in 2 soup cans of water and add celery, onions, and mushrooms. Cook on low heat for ¹/₂ hour or until venison is tender. Add store bought baked potato wedges and sweet corn - fresh corn if in season. Enjoy!

Y*ou will not be able to eat just one helping of this delightful venison Mexican dish. I know because I went back for seconds. Bake this ahead of time if you are trying to impress guests as they arrive. It fills the whole house with a delicious aroma. We made this dish as is but if fewer calories are desired, low fat cheese and low fat/no fat tortilla chips can be substituted. Thanks Debbie Carrol for sending us your recipe. It is delicious.*

DEBBIE'S MEXICAN CASSEROLE

You'll want a second helping!

1½ pounds ground venisonburger

1 large onion, chopped

2 cloves garlic, diced

salt and black pepper to taste

2 cans ranch-style beans

1 pkg. tortilla chips

2 cups shredded cheddar cheese

1 can cream of celery or broccoli soup

1 can cream of onion soup

1 can Rotel tomatoes with green chilies

Brown venison, onion and garlic in 3 teaspoons butter in a large frying pan. Salt and pepper to taste; add beans, stir, and turn off heat. Place a layer of chips in a buttered 9x13 inch casserole dish. Layer meat-bean mixture and cheese; top with layer of chips. Mix soups and tomatoes in a bowl; spoon over casserole. Bake at 350 degrees 30 minutes or until hot and bubbly.

FAMILY STYLE BREAKFAST VENISON CASSEROLE

1 pound venison bulk
  sausage
1/4 cup milk
6 eggs, beaten
salt and black pepper to taste
1 (8 oz.) pkg. cheddar cheese,
  shredded

1/4 teaspoon chili powder
2 sticks butter
12 slices bread, edges
  removed
1/4 cup Parmesan cheese

Brown venison sausage in skillet. In a bowl mix sausage, milk, eggs, salt, pepper, cheddar cheese, and chili powder. Melt one stick of butter and pour into bottom of 10 x 10 x 2 inch casserole dish. Coat both sides of 6 slices of bread with melted butter; arrange bread in bottom of dish. Pour mixed casserole ingredients over bread. Top with remaining slices of bread, coated with the remaining stick of butter, melted. Top with Parmesan cheese. Bake covered at 400 degrees for 20 minutes; uncovered, 5 minutes or until bread is browned and liquid is absorbed.

BRISTOL VENISON — "ITALIAN STYLE"

2 pounds venison steak,
  cubed small
1/2 cup olive oil
2 cloves garlic, minced
1 small onion, minced
2 (8 oz.) cans tomato sauce
1 bay leaf

1/2 teaspoon salt
2 teaspoons oregano
1/4 teaspoon black pepper
1 teaspoon Italian seasoning
1 (12 oz.) pkg. vermicelli
Parmesan cheese to taste

In a large, deep frying pan lightly brown cubed venison, garlic, and onion in olive oil. Add tomato sauce and remaining ingredients. Cover and simmer 1 1/2 hours or until venison is tender, stirring occasionally. When venison sauce is ready, cook vermicelli according to package directions; drain. Toss vermicelli with venison sauce and top with Parmesan cheese. Serve with home made spicy garlic bread.

BUCK'S VENISON MEAT PIE

Easy to make and even easier to eat.

1 (9 inch) pie shell
1 pound ground
  venisonburger
1 tablespoon butter
1/2 cup onion, chopped
1/2 cup bell pepper, diced
1 large clove garlic, diced
1/4 cup flour

1/2 cup black olives, chopped
1/4 cup salsa, mild or medium
generous dash of black
  pepper or hot sauce
1 (14 oz.) can stewed
  tomatoes, undrained
4 oz. can mushrooms, drained
1/2 teaspoon chili powder

Bake your pie shell as directed. Then brown ground venison in butter in skillet. Add onion, bell pepper and garlic; cook until pepper is tender. Add remaining ingredients, except pie shell; heat to boiling. Simmer 10 minutes and remove from heat. Spoon mixture into pie shell and bake in oven at 400 degrees for 25 minutes.

PONCHO'S FIESTA MEAT LOAF

This is an easy but tasty recipe for the young hunters around your house or deer camp to try. They will get plenty of complements at meal time!

1/2 cup chopped onion
1/2 cup chopped celery
2 tablespoons butter
1 teaspoon garlic powder
1 (16 oz.) bottle mild salsa
4 oz. can chopped green chili
  peppers, drained

1 1/2 pounds ground
  venisonburger
1 egg, slightly beaten
1/2 teaspoon salt
1 cup soft bread crumbs

Sauté onion and celery in butter, just until tender. Put in a bowl and stir in garlic powder, salsa, chili peppers, ground venison, egg, salt, and bread crumbs. Mix well and form into a loaf 8 x 4 x 1 1/2 in shallow baking pan. Bake in 350 degree oven for 1 to 1 1/2 hours. Let stand 5 minutes before slicing.

MISSISSIPPI BARBECUED VENISON STEAK FOR TWO

1½ pound venison round steak
1 cup flour
1 teaspoon salt

½ teaspoon black pepper
½ teaspoon garlic powder
½ teaspoon onion powder

SAUCE

1 cup salsa or picante sauce
2 teaspoons Worcestershire sauce
2 teaspoons butter

1½ cups water
1 teaspoon lemon juice
5-6 drops Tabasco sauce

Coat venison in seasoned flour of salt, pepper, garlic and onion powder, after cutting into serving size pieces. Fry lightly in small amount of butter. Place in 1½ quart casserole dish. Make sauce above in a small pan and then bring sauce to boil and pour on venison steak. Bake at 325 degree oven for 45 minutes to medium doneness. Serve with rice or baked potatoes. Good! This is a tasty venison steak any time of the year.

A MEMPHIS STYLE STEW

1 to 1½ pounds venisonburger or sausage
¾ cup green onions, chopped
1 small onion, chopped
2 green peppers, trimmed, seeded, and chopped
3 celery ribs, chopped

½ cup clam juice
salt and black pepper to taste
1 tablespoon marjoram
1 (10 oz.) pkg. frozen okra
1 pound raw shrimp, cleaned and deveined
cooked rice

In your Dutch oven brown venison 10 to 15 minutes and set aside. Place onions, green peppers, and celery in the Dutch oven. Add clam juice and enough water to cover plus the seasonings. Bring to a boil, reduce heat and simmer 10 minutes. Add venison and okra; cook 5 to 10 minutes, stirring occasionally. Add shrimp; cook 5 minutes longer. Remove pot from heat and let stand for 10 minutes. Serve over cooked rice. Add cocktail sauce or cayenne pepper to taste.

LAMONT'S MISSISSIPPI STYLE VENISON STEAK

1¹/₂ pounds venison steak, cubed

1 teaspoon salt

1¹/₂ teaspoons black pepper

2 cloves garlic, diced

1 large onion, chopped

1 large green bell pepper, chopped

1 cup bottled Italian salad dressing

¹/₄ cup vinegar

2 teaspoons Italian seasoning

3 fresh tomatoes, cut into fourths

¹/₂ cup grated Parmesan cheese

Spread cubed venison flat in 9 x 9 inch baking dish and sprinkle with salt and pepper; add pieces of garlic, onion and green pepper. Add Italian dressing, vinegar, Italian seasoning, and tomatoes. Marinate in refrigerator for 12 hours total turning venison once after 6 hours. Preheat oven to 350 degrees. Sprinkle venison with ¹/₂ cup Parmesan cheese. Cover and bake for 45 minutes. Then remove cover and bake 15 minutes more. Serve with rice and biscuits.

ROANOKE VIRGINIA ROAST OF VENISON

2 to 3 pound venison roast

2 teaspoons salt (divide usage)

1 teaspoon black pepper

3 cloves garlic, diced

1 tablespoon paprika

¹/₂ teaspoon chili powder

2 tablespoons Worcestershire sauce

1 cup chili sauce or catsup

2 tablespoon brown sugar

1 teaspoon dry mustard

¹/₂ teaspoon cayenne pepper

¹/₄ cup red wine or cider vinegar

¹/₂ cup water

Place venison roast in a roaster pan. Season with 1 teaspoon salt, pepper, and garlic. Roast in 350 degree oven 1 hour. Slice into thin slices. Mix remaining 1 teaspoonful salt with remaining ingredients in large skillet. Simmer 15 minutes. Add sliced venison and simmer about 1 hour, or until venison is tender. Excellent venison dish with sweet or baked potatoes and tossed salad.

CAJUN VENISON VEGETABLE CASSEROLE

2 pounds venison steak,
  sliced thin

1/2 cup butter

1/2 cup chopped onion

1/2 cup chopped red or green
  bell pepper

1/2 cup Italian bread crumbs

2 tablespoons water

2 teaspoons dried oregano

1 teaspoon ea. salt and chili
  powder

1 (10 oz.) pkg. frozen okra or
  broccoli, thawed

1/2 cup chopped carrots

3 eggs, slightly beaten

2 teaspoons ground cumin

1 cup Italian salad dressing

1/2 teaspoon cayenne pepper

Brown thinly sliced venison steak pieces in butter, 15 minutes or so. Heat oven to 350 degrees. Lightly spray 13 x 9 inch baking dish with no-stick cooking spray or grease lightly. In a large bowl combine steak and all ingredients; mix thoroughly. Place in prepared baking dish and bake 1 1/2 hours. Pass the mashed potatoes, please. Tasty! Yes, mam . . . . .

J. D. was the young owner of a local sporting goods store in Mississippi who was as country as they come. But did the man know about huntin' and fishin'! This good, easy recipe is named in his honor.

J. D.'s DELICIOUS VENISON STEAKS

3 tablespoons flour

1 teaspoon black pepper

1/4 teaspoon marjoram

2 pounds of venison steaks,
  cut from the round, hind
  quarter, cubed

1/2 cup butter

1 small onion, chopped

1/2 cup diced celery and tops

4 medium carrots, chopped

1 1/2 cups beef broth or
  1 (14 1/2 oz.) can of beef
  broth

Mix flour with pepper and marjoram; rub into venison. In a Dutch oven brown steaks in hot butter. Add vegetables and broth; cover and cook 45-60 minutes, or until steak is tender. Thicken liquid for gravy with flour and water. Stir to desired thickness. Great with sweet potatoes and corn.

*J*ohn Paul was an insurance agent friend of ours who
married a sweet woman named Debbie. Honestly,
John Paul was a character who could tell jokes
and stories with the best of the Southerners. Thanks
for your recipe, John Paul! This recipe is easy to
prepare and even easier to enjoy.

JOHN PAUL'S VENISON TACO PIE

1 deep dish or (9 inch) pie
crust, baked to pkg.
directions

1 pound venison sausage or
venisonburger

1 envelope (1¼ oz.) Taco
seasoning mix

1 jar (16 oz.) chunky picante
sauce, mild or medium

1 egg, beaten

1½ cups shredded Monterey
Jack cheese (divided usage)

1 can (4½ oz.) chopped green
chilies

⅓ cup broken tortilla chips

Bake your pie crust to package directions. In skillet, brown ground
venison. Add taco seasoning mix and 1 cup picante sauce, stir. Simmer 5 to 8 minutes; remove from heat. Stir in egg. Sprinkle prepared pie crust with ½ cup cheese; top with green chilies. Pour
ground venison mixture over chilies. Top with remaining 1 cup
cheese. Sprinkle tortilla chips over top. Bake in preheated 350 degree oven on preheated baking sheet 20 to 25 minutes. Serve along
with sour cream and remaining picante sauce. Tastes great!

BIG EASY SLOPPY JOES

1 pkg. (10 oz.) cornbread mix

1 pound ground
venisonburger

1 tablespoon butter

1 onion, cut into chunks

1/2 green pepper, cut into
chunks

2 cloves garlic, minced

1/2 teaspoon cayenne pepper

1 can (14 1/2 oz.) Cajun style
stewed tomatoes

1 can (8 oz.) tomato sauce

Prepare cornbread as package directs; cut into 6 pieces. In large pan, brown venison in butter with onion, green pepper, garlic, and cayenne pepper. Stir in tomatoes and tomato sauce. Season with salt and pepper to taste; stir. Simmer 15 minutes. Serve over cornbread or your favorite cooked rice.

This was a flavorful dish at deer camp for our hungry hunters. Some liked it moderately seasoned and others added even more tobassco sauce and cayenne pepper to their serving.

HUNGRY HUNTERS DIRTY RICE

1 pound ground
venisonburger

1 can onion soup

1 can cream of mushroom
soup

2 cloves garlic, diced

1 cup parsley, minced

1/2 cup chopped green bell
pepper

dash hot pepper sauce or
cayenne pepper

1 cup uncooked rice

1 cup chopped green onions

1/3 cup celery, chopped fine

1/3 cup finely chopped onion

red and black pepper to taste

In a large skillet brown your venison in a teaspoon butter. Add it to a three quart casserole dish. Then add all remaining ingredients. Cover the casserole dish with close-fitting cover in order to retain all the juices. Bake at 325 degrees for 1 hour. Then let set for 15 minutes before serving.

*W*e found this delicious venison dish easy to prepare. It had a flavorful aroma and serves four or more people. We strongly recommend you use some of your quality cared for venison when you give this recipe a try on your family or at hunting camp. Use additional cayenne pepper if you care to spice up individual dishes .... So good.

PONCHO'S VENISON OLE

1 pound venisonburger or steak, cut in small cubes

2 garlic cloves, diced

1 (11 oz.) can Mexican-style corn

1/2 bunch green onion, chopped

1 bell pepper, chopped

1 (15 1/2 oz.) can kidney beans

1/2 cup whole pitted olives, cut in half

1 cup salsa

1 (4 1/2 oz.) can green chili peppers

1 teaspoon salt

1 teaspoon basil leaves

1/2 teaspoon cayenne pepper

1 1/2 cups water

Brown venisonburger or small pieces of steak and garlic in a tablespoon of butter in a large frying pan 10 minutes or so. Add it to a 4-5 quart crockpot. Add vegetables, olives, salsa and chili peppers and stir. Now carefully add spices and water and blend well. Slow cook on high or 4-5 hours if you use steak or 3-4 hours if you use venisonburger. Recommend you serve this chili-like dish in bowls with corn bread.

CROCKERY
COOKING VENISON

*I*t is not necessary to sauté vegetables first for recipes. Just cut them and drop them in the crock and place seasoned meat on top of them. Add more seasoning and vegetables if called for.

The low moist heat of the crockery or slow cooker is ideal for tenderizing tougher cuts of venison like ribs, hocks and front shoulder roasts. Unlike in conventional cooking liquids do not cook away. So lean venison cooks up moist and tender. If you have a work day planned when using a crock pot recipe we suggest you prepare the meat and vegetables the night before and put the meal together the next morning before work.

Despite the venison's flavorful aroma during cooking, resist the temptation to lift the lid during cooking. It allows significant heat to escape so each time it extends the recipe cooking time.

Enjoy our recipes and never be afraid to experiment with your favorite seasonings or adding your favorite sauces or gravies. When you start a recipe with quality venison you can not go too far wrong ...

SMOKEY'S VENISON SLOPPY JOES

2 pounds venisonburger

2 tablespoons butter

1 large onion, chopped

3 cloves garlic, minced

1 teaspoon oregano

1 envelope spaghetti sauce
  mix

1 (18 oz.) can tomato juice

1 (1 pound) can whole kernel
  corn

1 cup chopped celery or
  carrots

1 cup salsa, mild or medium

Heat butter in skillet and brown venison. Combine all ingredients in slow cooker, stirring well. Cook on low heat 6 to 8 hours, or on high heat 3 to 4 hours. Serve on buns or rolls of your choice.

LOCK PIT VENISON DINNER

1 pound cooked venison
  roast, cut into 1 inch cubes

1 medium onion, sliced

1/2 cup uncooked rice

1 1/2 teaspoons salt

1 teaspoon garlic powder

1 tablespoon soy sauce

1 tablespoon Worcestershire
  sauce

1 (1 pound) can tomatoes,
  with juice

1 cup water

1/2 teaspoon pepper

1 tablespoon chili powder

Combine all ingredients in slow cooker. Cook on high 3 to 4 hours, or on automatic 4 to 5 hours. You can vary this dish by using venisonburger or sausage. ENJOY!

EASY DEER CAMP VENISON ROAST

4 tablespoons flour
1 tablespoon salt
1/2 teaspoon black pepper
2 1/2 to 3 pounds venison roast
4 tablespoons butter
2 large white onions, sliced

1 pound potatoes, quartered
6 carrots, sliced
3 stalks celery, chopped
10-14 oz. can beef bouillon
1 cup dry red wine
2 medium tomatoes, chopped

Mix together flour, salt, and black pepper and coat venison with mixture. Heat butter in a large skillet and brown venison roast. Combine all ingredients in slow cooker. Cook on low heat 7 to 8 hours, or on high 5 to 6 hours.

MERIDIAN VENISON BARBECUE

2 tablespoons butter
1 1/2 pounds venison, cubed small
3/4 cup chopped onion
1/2 cup diced celery
1/2 green pepper, chopped
2 cloves garlic, minced
1 tablespoon Worcestershire sauce
1/2 cup catsup

1/4 teaspoon red pepper flakes
1 teaspoon salt
1/2 teaspoon chili powder
1/2 teaspoon black pepper
6 oz. can tomato paste
3/4 cup water
2 tablespoons vinegar
2 teaspoons brown sugar
1 teaspoon dry mustard

Heat butter in skillet and brown venison. Combine venison and all ingredients in slow cooker, stirring well. Cook on low heat 6 to 8 hours, or on high heat 4 to 5 hours. Serve on hamburger buns or over rice or noodles. You will be back for seconds either way, guaranteed!!

THE BURG'S VENISON CASSEROLE

**2 pounds venison stew meat
or deer hocks, cut into
2 inch cubes**
2 medium onions, sliced
1 1/2 teaspoons salt
1/2 teaspoon black pepper
3/4 cup dry red wine

**10.5 oz. can condensed beef
consommé**
**10.5 oz. can golden
mushroom soup**
1/2 cup fine dry bread crumbs
1/2 cup flour

Brown your venison in 3 tablespoons butter and put it in a slow cooker, along with all ingredients except bread crumbs and flour. Stir. Blend crumbs with flour and add to cooker. Cook on high heat 5 to 6 hours, or on automatic 7 hours. Ah, now serve with a favorite vegetable and a tossed salad. A deliciously nutritious meal for your family.

BUCK GRUNT VENISON PASTA SAUCE

2 pounds venison stew meat
2 tablespoons butter
1 cup chopped onion
1 cup chopped green pepper
2 cloves garlic, diced
**1 cup chopped fresh
mushrooms**
1 teaspoon chili powder

2 (28 oz.) cans tomatoes
1 (6 oz.) can tomato paste
2 teaspoons salt
3 teaspoons oregano
1/2 teaspoon parsley
**1/2 teaspoon Italian
seasoning**
1/2 teaspoon black pepper

In a large skillet brown venison in butter for 15 minutes. Combine all ingredients in slow cooker, stirring well. Cook on low heat 7 to 8 hours, on high heat 5 to 6 hours, or on automatic 6 to 7 hours. Enjoy this venison sauce over any of your favorite pasta. Freeze leftovers, of course, for other great Italian meals.

DEER TRAIL VENISON STEAK

2 pounds venison steak, cut in ¹/₂ inch pieces

4 tablespoons butter

1 medium onion, chopped

1 teaspoon salt

¹/₂ teaspoon pepper

¹/₂ teaspoon thyme

¹/₂ teaspoon Italian seasoning

¹/₂ teaspoon marjoram

2 tablespoons chopped parsley

1 (14 oz.) can beef stock

¹/₂ pound sliced smoked sausage or kilbasa

1 (4 oz.) can mushrooms, drained

¹/₄ cup bread crumbs

Brown venison in butter 15 minutes or so. Combine venison, onion, and seasonings in slow cooker. Pour in beef stock, sausage, mushrooms, and bread crumbs. Cook on low heat 8 hours, or on high heat 4 to 5 hours. Serve with baked potatoes. Enjoy!

CINDY'S VENISON STUFFED PEPPERS

1 tablespoon butter

1 pound venisonburger or sausage

1 cup cooked rice

1 small onion, chopped

1 teaspoon salt

¹/₂ teaspoon black pepper

¹/₂ teaspoon basil

¹/₂ cup chili or picante sauce

6 medium green peppers, tops removed and seeded

8 oz. can tomato sauce

¹/₄ cup Romano or Parmesan cheese

Heat butter in skillet and brown venison. Combine venison and next six ingredients in bowl. Stuff green peppers about two-thirds full. Arrange peppers in slow cooker, with two or three on bottom and others placed above them. (Sprinkle left-over stuffing on top.) Pour tomato sauce into slow cooker. Top with Romano or Parmesan cheese. Cook on low heat 5 to 6 hours, or on high heat 3 to 4 hours. Tasty and good for you, too!

SHOTGUN VENISON AND RICE CASSEROLE

1 pound ground
  venisonburger
2 tablespoons butter
1 small onion, thinly sliced
1/2 cup sliced celery or
  carrots
1/2 teaspoon oregano

1 can condensed cream of
  chicken soup
1 teaspoon soy sauce
1 teaspoon Worcestershire or
  steak sauce
1 cup cooked rice

Heat butter in skillet and brown venison. Combine all ingredients except rice in slow cooker. Cook on high 3 hours. Add cooked rice. Cook 30 minutes more; then enjoy!

We hope you find these and our other crockpot recipes delicious. They are easy to prepare and always nutritious. You've got to try this one!

ACROSS THE BORDER VENISON CASSEROLE

1 1/2 pounds venison
  sausage or venisonburger
2 tablespoons butter
1 medium onion, chopped
2/3 cup chopped celery
1 cup grated Cheddar cheese

1 (8 oz.) can tomato sauce or
  salsa
1 1/2 teaspoons chili powder
1/2 teaspoon oregano
2 (1 pound) cans pork and
  beans or beans of choice

Brown venison in heated butter. Combine it and all ingredients in slow cooker, stirring well. Cook on low heat 4 to 6 hours. Serve as is or over noodles or rice. May I have seconds, please!

CROSS BOW VENISON CORN CASSEROLE

1 pound venison steak, cubed
2 tablespoons olive oil
1 medium onion, sliced very thin
1 teaspoon salt
1/2 teaspoon black pepper
2 teaspoons Worcestershire sauce

1 can condensed cream of celery or onion soup
1 soup can water
1 (1 pound) can cream-style corn
2 cups (about half an 8 oz. pkg.) egg noodles
1 teaspoon chopped parsley

Heat olive oil in skillet and brown venison. Combine venison and all ingredients except noodles and parsley in slow cooker. Cook on high heat 3-4 hours. Add noodles and parsley and cook until done; about 15 minutes.

VENISONBURGER STROGANOFF

1 pound ground venisonburger
2 tablespoons butter
2 medium onions, chopped
2 cloves garlic, minced
1/2 pound mushrooms, sliced
1 teaspoon salt

1/2 teaspoon black pepper
1 tablespoon Worcestershire sauce
3 tablespoons tomato paste
1/3 cup dry red wine
1 cup beef broth
1 cup sour cream

Brown venisonburger in heated butter. Combine all ingredients except sour cream in slow cooker. Cook on low heat 6 to 8 hours. Before serving, add sour cream to slow cooker and stir well. Heat 30 minutes, and serve over egg noodles.

GALE'S QUICK VENISON SWISS STEAK

2 pounds venison round steak, cut into serving pieces

1 teaspoon salt

1/2 teaspoon black pepper

1/2 teaspoon parsley

2 cloves garlic, diced

1/2 teaspoon red pepper flakes

1 large onion, sliced (or 1 pkg. onion- soup mix)

1 (16 oz.) can tomatoes

1 teaspoon Italian seasoning

1 teaspoon soy sauce

Combine all ingredients in slow cooker. Cook on low heat 6 to 8 hours or on high heat 5 to 6 hours. Add a sweet or baked Idaho potato for a tasty meal.

BUCK IN HEAT VENISON STEW WITH BEER

Try me, please, you will be very glad you did.

1/4 cup flour

1 teaspoon salt

1/2 teaspoon black pepper

2 pounds venison stew meat or 4 hocks, cut into 1 inch cubes

3 slices bacon, diced

1 can beer

2 tablespoons soy sauce

2 tablespoons Worcestershire sauce

1 teaspoon Italian seasoning

1/2 teaspoon crumbled bay leaves

3 cloves garlic, crushed

1 large onion, sliced

1 pound mushrooms, sliced

Mix flour, salt and black pepper together and coat venison cubes with mixture. Fry bacon bits until crisp; discard fat. In a bowl mix together beer, soy and Worcestershire sauce, and remaining seasonings. Place venison, bacon, garlic, onions, and mushrooms in slow cooker. Pour liquid mixture over them. Cook on low heat 8-10 hours or on high heat 6-7 hours.

We love to prepare our quality cared for venison in crock pot recipes. These recipes can not miss. Just taste and you will see smiles all around the table.

STEELER'S VENISON ROUND STEAK

2 tablespoons butter

2 pounds venison steak, cubed

1/2 large onion, chopped

2 cloves garlic, minced

1/2 cup chopped mushrooms

1/4 cup chopped parsley

1 1/2 cups soft bread crumbs

2 tablespoons Worcestershire sauce

1 teaspoon poultry seasoning

1/2 teaspoon salt

1/2 teaspoon pepper

1 egg, slightly beaten

1/2 cup water or bouillon

In a skillet heat the butter; add venison, onion, and garlic, and sauté until lightly browned. Place the browned venison mixture in slow cooker along with remaining ingredients. Stir well. Cook on low heat 8 to 10 hours, or on automatic 6 to 7 hours. Add asparagus and baked potato. Enjoy!

STEVE'S SAVORY BUCK ROAST & GRAVY

1 1/2 to 2 pounds venison roast

1/2 cup chopped carrots

3 cloves garlic, diced

1/8 teaspoon ground cloves

1/2 cup chopped onion

4 tablespoons parsley

1 (18 oz.) jar Heinz savory beef gravy

1 1/2 teaspoons black pepper

Place your venison roast in a 3 to 4 quart slow cooker. Then put remaining ingredients in a bowl. Mix and pour over your venison roast. Cover; cook on low heat for 8 to 10 hours or on high setting for 5 to 6 hours. Add a baked potato and a favorite vegetable for a nutritious main meal.

*T his tasty venison dish was served to us hungry
hunters once a deer season at least while
hunting the Arliss farm in upstate New York.
Thanks for your recipe, Ella.*

ELLA'S CROCKPOT VENISON

2¹/₂ to 3 pound venison roast
6 garlic cloves, diced

2 medium or 1 large onion, sliced in half
1 teaspoon seasoned salt

Boil venison in water along with the above ingredients for 45 minutes. Then put your venison in a 3¹/₂ quart or larger crock pot and add:

1 green pepper, sliced
1 cup red wine - Burgundy (dry) or Rosé (sweet)
1¹/₂ teaspoons seasoned salt
1 teaspoon Italian seasoning
1 can cream of celery soup

1 can of beer
1 teaspoon red pepper (optional)
1 teaspoon black pepper
1¹/₂ teaspoons garlic powder
1 can golden mushroom soup

Make sure your roast is covered with seasonings and soup. Slow cook on high for 3 to 4 hours or on low for 4 to 5 hours until venison is tender. Serve with rice and a favorite vegetable.

*Hungry hunters or family members will come running once they have tried this dish. Its gotta be a favorite recipe for you ..... Enjoy!

A DEER HUNTER'S WIFE KNOWS!
Even though my husband may enjoy preparing tasty venison dishes for family and friends, I have my own special venison recipes I like to prepare year in and year out. My favorite recipes in Quality Venison II *will make you a believer about cooking healthy, savory venison meals for your family's dinner table, too.*

*I*f you have been looking for the way to enjoy venison ribs you have just found your recipe. You will like the slight sweetness in the barbecue sauce because of the chili sauce and Rosé wine.

CROCK POT BARBECUE VENISON RIBS

2 to 2¹/₂ pounds venison ribs, cut into 6-8 inch squares

1 pound link smoked sausage or kilbassa, sliced thin

¹/₂ stick butter

1 teaspoon Worcestershire sauce

15-16 oz. can stewed tomatoes

2 stalks celery, chopped

¹/₂ cup onions, chopped

1 green pepper, sliced

1 teaspoon liquid smoke (optional)

¹/₄ cup lemon juice

1 teaspoon chili powder

¹/₂ cup catsup or chili sauce

¹/₂ teaspoon oregano

1 teaspoon Italian seasoning

1 teaspoon garlic powder

1 teaspoon dry mustard

1 teaspoon salt

³/₄ cup Rosé wine - *Important**

Bake ribs at 400 degrees for 20-30 minutes; turn ribs and pour off grease after 15 minutes. (This baking time melts the fat off the ribs to eliminate potential for a strong flavor to the finished rib dish). After 30 minutes remove ribs and add to 3-4 quart crock pot along with sliced smoked sausage or kilbassa. Make barbecue sauce while the ribs are baking in a medium sauce pan by adding remaining ingredients. Simmer until ribs are done baking. Add barbecue sauce to crock pot. Cook on high for 6 hours or low for 8 hours. Rice goes great with this rib dish. Great recipe for a cold January indoor picnic.

T his recipe is a tasty, time saving way to make a nutritious pot of venison and vegetable soup almost from scratch.

NO FUSS VENISON & VEGETABLE SOUP

1 to 1½ pounds venison
 stew meat, cubed small

8 cups water

1 canister Wyler's Vegetable
 Beef soup starter

1 (10 oz.) pkg. frozen mixed
 vegetables

1 teaspoon chili powder

3 fresh garlic gloves, diced

1 cup green onions, chopped

1 cup beef gravy or beef
 bouillon

1 (14½ oz.) can stewed
 tomatoes

In a frying pan brown venison in two tablespoons olive oil ten minutes or so. Then add to the crock pot. Add water, Vegetable Beef soup starter, frozen mixed vegetables, and chili powder. Dice garlic, chop onions; add them, the gravy or bouillon, and stewed tomatoes to crock pot and stir well. Cover and cook on high for 4 to 5 hours. Serve with bread or biscuits. So - so - good!

Cooking Venison
Italian Style

Our family is Italian and because of our heritage and the restaurant business we have always loved Italian food. Many years ago when I would be "in the mood" for an Italian dish I began substituting venison for beef and venison sausage for pork sausage in Italian dishes I would prepare. We found the rich flavor of venison added a savory, robust flavor to Italian dishes, and venison lasagna is the family favorite. We know you will enjoy these savory, nutritious dishes.

Steve prepared this different pasta dish using his home made venison bulk sausage for our family and we all loved it. It will serve 6 to 8, too. Freeze leftovers. Don't be afraid. Served after freezing it tastes great, too ....

STEVE'S VENISON BOW TIE PASTA

12 oz. bow tie pasta

1 pound venisonburger or sausage

3/4 cup chopped onion

2 to 3 garlic cloves, diced

1 (28-32 oz.) jar your favorite pasta sauce

1/2 teaspoon black pepper

24 oz. Ricotta cheese

1 cup milk

1 teaspoon salt

1 cup Romano or Mozzarella cheese

2 tablespoons grated Parmesan cheese

First cook the bow tie pasta to package directions. While pasta is cooking, sauté venison, onion, and garlic in a Dutch oven, over medium heat 10 minutes or so, until venison is nicely browned. To it add jar of pasta sauce and black pepper. Simmer for 10 minutes more. Then stir in Ricotta cheese, milk, and salt. Stir well and simmer 10 minutes. Add pasta and Romano or Mozzarella cheese to Dutch oven and stir well. Spoon pasta mixture into a 9 x 13 x 2 inch baking dish. Sprinkle top with Parmesan cheese and bake at 350 degrees for 20 minutes or until heated through. Delicious for sure! This dish can be made ahead and frozen until used. Thaw it out over 24 hours in refrigerator. Then bake at 350 degrees for 45 to 60 minutes. That's Italian!

*T*his special venison sauce makes 6 quarts so you may want to halve the recipe for smaller occasions. Mom's Venison Pasta Sauce is thick and savory. Add water if a thinner sauce is preferred. Top off your meal with toasted garlic bread and your favorite red wine for a special Italian meal, and the Olive Garden Restaurant cannot compare!

MOM'S VENISON PASTA SAUCE

2 cups chopped onion

10-12 chopped green onions (including the tops)

6 garlic cloves, diced

2 stalks celery, chopped

2 tablespoons olive oil

1 pound venisonburger

1/2 pound bulk venison or pork sausage

2 teaspoons sugar

1 cup red wine

3 (28 oz.) cans tomato sauce

1-2 (28 oz.) cans water

2 teaspoons Italian seasoning

1 teaspoon oregano

2 teaspoons basil

1 teaspoon red pepper flakes (optional)

2 bay leaves

To a large frying pan or Dutch oven add chopped onions, diced garlic and chopped celery. Add olive oil, venisonburger and sausage. Stir well and brown for 20 minutes, stirring occasionally. Drain oil if necessary before adding to a 6 quart slow cooker. Stir and add sugar, red wine, tomato sauce, water as needed and last 5 seasoning ingredients. Stir well and slow cook on low setting 6-8 hours or on high for 4-5 hours. Serve over your favorite pasta to 8-10 hungry hunters or guests.

This is an easy, quick recipe that will please just about any family member or friends you are having for dinner.

CHUNKY VENISON PASTA BAKE

6-8 oz. uncooked penne or other tube pasta

1 pound venison steak, sliced thin

1 small onion, chopped

2 cloves garlic, minced

2 tablespoons olive oil

1 can (10¾ oz.) condensed golden mushroom soup

1 can (14½ oz.) chunky pasta style stewed tomatoes

1½ cups mozzarella cheese, shredded

Cook pasta as package directs; drain and place in a large bowl. In skillet, brown venison with onion and garlic in olive oil. Combine venison mixture with pasta, add mushroom soup, and tomatoes; place in 7 x 11 inch baking dish. Cover and bake at 350 degrees, 25 minutes. Uncover; top with mozzarella cheese. Bake 5 minutes longer or until cheese is melted.

ROG'S PEPPY VENISON PASTA

1 pound venison steak, sliced in thin strips

1 cup onion, chopped

2 cloves garlic, minced

8 ounces your favorite pasta

3 to 4 ounces thinly sliced pepperoni

28 oz. jar pasta sauce, your favorite

1 cup fresh mushrooms, sliced

1 tablespoon Italian seasoning

3 ounces black olives, sliced

2 tablespoons grated Parmesan cheese

4 ounces shredded Mozzarella cheese

Brown your venison steak (venisonburger or venison sausage could be substituted also) with onion and garlic in 2 tablespoons olive oil. In a 9 x 13 inch baking dish add venison and combine remaining ingredients except Mozzarella cheese. Sprinkle Mozzarella cheese over top of pasta dish. Cover and bake at 350 degrees for 45 minutes. Uncover and bake 5 to 10 minutes to brown and melt cheese. Nutritiously delicious with garlic bread and fresh tossed green salad. Enjoy!

*Y*ou will want to try this easy and very tasty pasta
sauce for yourself, soon. We had it with friends
recently and they raved about it. Though it is not
prepared with all fresh ingredients, enough are fresh that
you can not tell it is not made completely from scratch.
This truly is a short cut recipe to a delicious pasta sauce.
Let us know what you think.

GALE'S SHORT CUT PASTA SAUCE

1¹/₂ pound of venison steak or
stew meat, cubed small

2 cloves garlic, diced

3 green onions, chopped

2 medium tomatoes, chopped

1 cup fresh mushrooms,
sliced

2 cups salsa, mild or medium

1 (26-32 oz.) jar of pasta sauce

2 cups water

¹/₂ cup Parmesan cheese

In a frying pan brown cubed venison in olive oil, 10 minutes or so.
Add it and remaining ingredients to a 4 to 5 quart slow cooker. Turn
on high and cook your sauce 5 to 6 hours. Serve this savory pasta
sauce over your favorite pasta cooked to package directions.

 *It was years and years ago that Steve would cre-
atively "throw a recipe together" from whatever
ingredients he had on hand. The dish was always
delicious but he could never duplicate it because he
did not write any of it down. After my repeated
encouragement he finally started his own recipe
creations by writing down the ingredients and instructions. Many of these are now in our* Quality Venison I
& II *cookbooks for you to enjoy. --Gale Loder*

*I*n the summer time when home grown fresh zucchini is abundant, this is one of our favorite venison pasta dishes. The salsa will give you the taste you are looking for. You have to try this one!

LODER'S RESTAURANT VENISON ITALIANO

8 oz. favorite pasta

1 pound ground venisonburger

1 tablespoon olive oil

1 clove garlic, diced

1/2 medium onion, chopped

1 teaspoon Italian seasoning, crushed

1 (14 1/2 oz.) can stewed tomatoes

8 oz. mild or medium salsa

2 (8 oz.) cans tomato sauce

1 medium carrot, chopped

2 medium zucchini, cubed

1 cup water

Cook pasta as package directs; drain. In skillet, brown venison in olive oil with garlic, onion and Italian seasoning. Add tomatoes, salsa, tomato sauce and carrots. Cook, uncovered, over medium heat 8 minutes or so, stirring occasionally. Add zucchini and water; cover and cook 10 minutes or until zucchini is tender. Serve venison sauce over your pasta.

DAD'S VENISON STUFFED SHELLS

A delicious dish to satisfy your hungry family or when entertaining family or friends.

1 pkg. (9 oz.) jumbo macaroni shells for filling
1 1/2 pounds ground venison or venison sausage
2 cups (8 oz.) shredded cheese of your choice
3/4 teaspoon garlic salt
1/2 teaspoon black pepper

1 egg
1 cup bread crumbs
1 teaspoon Italian seasoning
1/2 cup steak sauce
3 cups tomato juice
1 (8 oz.) can tomato sauce
1/2 cup Parmesan cheese

In 4 quarts boiling salted water, cook shells 9 to 10 minutes. Drain. Rinse with cold water. In large skillet, brown venison until crumbly. To the skillet mix in shredded cheese, garlic salt, black pepper, egg, bread crumbs, Italian seasoning and steak sauce. Stuff shells with meat mixture. Pour one half juice in bottom of 9 x 13 x 2 inch baking pan. Arrange stuffed shells in single layer in pan. Pour remaining juice over all, and top with tomato sauce. Sprinkle with Parmesan cheese. Bake in preheated 350 degree oven 35 to 40 minutes or until lightly browned and bubbly. That is Italian, Ah!

A DEER HUNTER'S WIFE KNOWS!

Ways to "Share the Harvest"—over the years we have had a habit of sharing our venison with neighbors, relatives or friends. It is our way of dispelling the old adage that venison is "gamy." We will often make a big Dutch oven of venison stew, chili, soup, or pasta sauce, etc. and freeze it in give-away plastic containers. When the opportunity comes around for us to share our tasty venison dishes, we do and it is always much appreciated.

We also hope wives encourage their deer hunting husbands that when they are blessed with a bountiful deer hunting season that they consider sharing their venison with local area food banks who are charitably feeding the less fortunate people in communities all over the country.

*T*his tasty recipe is one that inexperienced cooks or young hunters should try and prepare so they can make a good impression and get tall praise. Give it a try.

BUCK TRAIL VENISON PASTA SAUCE

1 pound ground
  venisonburger or sausage
1 tablespoon butter
1/2 medium onion, coarsely
  chopped
2 cloves garlic, minced
1 teaspoon Italian seasoning

2 cans (14 1/2 oz. ea.) chunky
  style stewed tomatoes
1 can (8 oz.) tomato sauce
1/4 cup red wine - *not cooking
  wine*
hot cooked pasta
grated Parmesan or Romano
  cheese

In large sauce pan, brown venison in butter 10 minutes or so. Add onion, garlic, and Italian seasoning; stir. Add chunky tomatoes, tomato sauce, and wine; blend well. Cook, uncovered over medium heat 25 minutes, stirring frequently. Prepare pasta as package directs. Serve sauce over pasta and top with Parmesan or Romano cheese to taste.

DAD'S VENISON ITALIANO

*Serving size for 4. Prepare
  pasta or your favorite rice.
1 pound venison steak, cut
  into thin strips
2 tablespoons olive oil
1 onion, cut into chunks
1 carrot, sliced
2 cloves garlic, crushed

1 can (14 1/2 oz.) Italian style
  stewed tomatoes
1 can (10 3/4 oz.) condensed
  cream of mushroom soup or
  other cream soup of your
  choice
1 cup Italian green or
  garbonzo beans

Prepare rice or pasta to package directions and set aside. In large skillet, cook venison in oil over high heat, stirring constantly until brown. Remove; set aside. To skillet, add onion, carrot and garlic; cook 2 minutes. Stir in tomatoes and soup; cover and simmer 10 minutes. Uncover; stir in beans. Cook over medium heat 20 minutes, stirring frequently. Add venison back; heat through 10 minutes. Serve over hot cooked pasta, rice, or wide egg noodles.

Sue's Simple Venison Lasagna

Make this meal ahead of time, and then serve for a special meal. Your family will want seconds. Who made the garlic bread?

8 uncooked lasagna noodles

1 pound ground venisonburger

3 tablespoons steak sauce

1 jar (32 oz.) spaghetti sauce

1 teaspoon garlic powder

1 teaspoon onion flakes

2 cups (16 oz.) ricotta cheese

2 cups (8 oz.) shredded mozzarella cheese

1 cup (4 oz.) Parmesan cheese

Cook lasagna noodles according to package directions, and drain. In large skillet, brown venison until crumbly. Mix steak sauce, spaghetti sauce, garlic powder, and onion flakes; stir. Cover bottom of 9 x 13 inch baking pan with sauce mixture (approximately 1/3 of total amount). Layer 1/3 of the lasagna, 1/2 of the ricotta, 1/3 of the venison, 1/3 of the mozzarella and 1/3 of the Parmesan cheese. Repeat. End with lasagna, venison, sauce, mozzarella and Parmesan. Bake in preheated 350 degree oven 45 minutes. Allow to stand 15 minutes before serving. Delicious with green salad and a glass of your favorite red wine.

*T*his recipe was easy to prepare and delicious when
we used a pound of our home made venison
sausage, but venison sausage of your choice will, of
course, be just fine. Drain fat from pan if necessary after
browning. It is a really nutritious winter-warmer,
so give it a try on your family.

ITALIAN STYLE VENISON & BEAN SOUP

1 pound venisonburger or
  sausage
2 garlic cloves, minced
1 stalk celery, chopped
1 cup onions, chopped
2 teaspoons olive oil
1 teaspoon Italian seasoning
1/2 teaspoon parsley
1/2 teaspoon basil or chives
1 (28 oz.) can stewed
  tomatoes

3 1/2 cups water
2 beef bouillon cubes
1 cup small pasta shells,
  uncooked
1 (16-18 oz.) can garbonzo or
  Italian green beans
1/2 teaspoon red pepper flakes
  (optional)
1/4 cup Parmesan cheese

In a Dutch oven brown the venison with garlic, celery, and onions
in olive oil 10 minutes or so. Add Italian seasoning, parsley, basil or
chives and stewed tomatoes; stir. Cook 10-15 minutes; then add
water and bouillon and bring to a boil; add pasta, beans, red pepper
and cheese; reduce heat; cover and simmer 20-30 minutes. Nutritiously delicious — Guaranteed!

*T*his recipe was recently prepared for our holiday office party of six. It smelled so good the ladies who do not eat venison had to try it anyway. Not much was left over even though it feeds eight. Mom was right when she said that even for lasagna it was simple to prepare. Enjoy one of our favorite pasta dishes.

Mom's Luscious Venison Lasagna

1 pound venisonburger or sausage

2 cloves garlic, minced

3 tablespoons parsley

1 teaspoon dried basil, crushed

1 (14^1/$_2$ oz.) can tomatoes, cut up

1 (8 oz.) can tomato sauce

1 (6 oz.) can tomato paste

10 oz. lasagna noodles (about 10 noodles)

3 cups Ricotta cheese

2 eggs, beaten

^{1}/$_4$ to ^{1}/$_2$ teaspoon black pepper

1 cup grated Parmesan cheese

8 oz. shredded mozzarella cheese

1 teaspoon Italian seasoning

In a large saucepan cook venison until brown. Add garlic, 1 tablespoon parsley, basil, undrained tomatoes, tomato sauce, and tomato paste to venison. Bring just to boiling; reduce heat. Simmer, uncovered, for 10 to 15 minutes or until thickened, stirring occasionally. Meanwhile, cook noodles according to package directions; drain. Rinse with cold water. Drain the noodles well. In a bowl combine Ricotta cheese, eggs, black pepper, remaining 2 tablespoons parsley, and 1/2 cup Parmesan cheese.

Arrange half the noodles in a 3-quart rectangular baking dish. Spread with half the Ricotta cheese mixture. Sprinkle with half the mozzarella cheese. Spoon half the meat mixture over all. Repeat layers. On top sprinkle with additional 1/2 cup Parmesan cheese and Italian seasoning. Bake in a 375 degree oven for 30 minutes or until heated through. Let stand 10 to 15 minutes before serving then the lasagna is easier to cut and serve.

SIS'S VENISON GARDEN SAUTÉ

8 oz. favorite pasta
1 pound venison steak, thinly
  sliced
2 teaspoons olive oil
1/2 teaspoon oregano
1 teaspoon salt
1/2 teaspoon black pepper
1 can (14.5 oz.) Italian stewed
  tomatoes
1/2 teaspoon parsley

1 green pepper, cut in thin
  strips
1 medium zucchini, cut in
  3 inch thin strips
18 small black ripe pitted
  olives
1 large carrot, cut in 3 inch
  thin strips
1 (6 oz.) can tomato paste or 1
  cup salsa

Cook pasta according to package directions and drain. In skillet brown venison in olive oil for 10 minutes. Then sprinkle with oregano, salt and pepper; stir. Add remaining ingredients; bring to boil. Cover and cook 5 minutes over medium heat. Uncover; cook over medium-high heat 8-10 minutes or until thickened. Serve hot over our favorite pasta. Everyone likes Italian food, and rich tasting venison make Italian dishes even better.

SAVORY BURGUNDY VENISON LINGUINI

8 oz. linguini pasta
1 pound venison steak, very
  thinly sliced
2 cloves garlic, minced
1/2 teaspoon thyme
2 teaspoons olive oil

1/4 pound fresh mushrooms,
  sliced
1 can (14 1/2 oz.) Italian style
  stewed tomatoes
1 can (8 oz.) tomato sauce
3/4 cup Burgundy wine

Cook pasta as package directs; drain. Meanwhile, sauté venison, garlic and thyme in hot olive oil 5 minutes. Add mushrooms; cook 5 minutes. Add tomatoes, tomato sauce and wine. Cook, uncovered, over medium heat 25 minutes, stirring occasionally. Serve over linguini. Now that's Italian!

STEVE'S VENISON FETTUCCINE WITH TRICOLOR PEPPERS

1 (12 oz.) pkg. fettuccine

1 pound venison steak, thinly sliced in small pieces

2 tablespoons olive oil

2 garlic cloves, diced

1 teaspoon Italian seasoning

1 cup each green, red and yellow sweet peppers, chopped

1/2 medium onion, chopped

1 1/2 cups your favorite store bought gravy

In a Dutch oven, boil fettuccine and drain as package directs. Lightly season the venison steak with salt and pepper. In a skillet fry your lightly seasoned venison steak in olive oil with garlic and Italian seasoning until brown, 10 to 12 minutes or so. Then add chopped green, red, and yellow sweet peppers, and onion. Cook 5 to 7 minutes. Mix gravy with drained fettuccine in Dutch oven and add your venison mixture. Stir well and serve immediately with Parmesan cheese and red pepper flakes to taste. Add a tossed salad and garlic bread for a delicious *Italian Style* meal!

 A DEER HUNTER'S WIFE KNOWS!

A hunter's venison from the whitetail deer is to be appreciated and never wasted because the deer is a gift from God. The main objective of the writing of our two Quality Venison *cookbooks is to dispel the "myth" that venison has a gamy taste. It is the spoiled fat when left on venison and frozen, that gives venison a gamy flavor. "Quality Venison" carefully field dressed and hand processed is never "gamy."*

*W*e *found this recipe delicious and simple to prepare. It is an appetizing dish to serve your family because of the golden brown chees topping. It makes plenty so we shared some with our new neighbors, Ray and Kim. They too said it was simply delicious!*

CLASSIC BAKED VENISON PASTA

12 oz. of favorite pasta
2 (20 oz.) jars pasta sauce
1 pound bulk venison
   sausage or venisonburger
2 garlic cloves, diced

¹/₄ cup oregano
4 cups shredded mozzarella
   cheese
¹/₄ cup chopped parsley

Preheat oven to 350 degrees. Prepare pasta as directed. Combine all ingredients, except parsley and using only two cups of cheese in large bowl, mixing well. Pour into greased 13 x 9 baking dish. Cover with foil. Bake about 45 minutes or until hot and bubbly. Uncover, top with remaining 2 cups cheese and parsley. Bake 10 minutes longer before serving ... AH!

DAD'S VENISON & EGGPLANT PARMESAN

So - So - Good . . . . . .

1¹/₂ pounds eggplant, cut in ¹/₄ inch slices

2 quarts salted water

1 pound venisonburger or sausage

1 cup onion, chopped

3 garlic cloves, diced

1 tablespoon olive oil

2 (8 oz.) cans tomato sauce

1¹/₂ cups salsa, chili, or picante sauce

¹/₂ teaspoon black pepper

1 teaspoon Italian seasoning

2¹/₂ cups shredded Mozzarella cheese

¹/₂ cup grated Parmesan cheese

In a Dutch oven cook eggplant in salted water until just tender; drain. Place on paper towels to absorb extra moisture. Using Dutch oven brown venison with onion and garlic 10 minutes or so in olive oil. Stir in tomato sauce, salsa, chili or mild picante sauce, black pepper and Italian seasoning. Then simmer 10 minutes and preheat oven to 350 degrees. Spray a 2¹/₂ quart casserole baking dish with non-stick spray and layer half the eggplant, half the venison sauce, 1¹/₂ cups mozzarella and 2 tablespoons Parmesan cheese in the casserole dish. Repeat layers with remaining ingredients, topping with Parmesan cheese. Bake for 40 to 45 minutes. Makes 5 to 6 servings. That's Italian. Enjoy with wild rice or sweet potatoes.

Any cut of venison from the whitetail deer whether from the treasured tenderloin, the hind quarter, or front shoulder, when it has been quality cared for after a clean one shot kill, carefully aged and boned, all fat trimmed and removed before freezing, and double freezer wrapped is as delicious as it is nutritious. My husband has been carefully doing it this way for over twenty-five years and our family has never had a "gamy" venison meal.

—Gale Loder

*R*ick's Spicy Venison Sauce was especially delicious when we served it to friends over cheese filled raviolis. What we really like about preparing venison pasta sauce is it allows us to freeze leftover sauce for future no fuss special pasta meals any time.

RICK'S SPICY VENISON SAUCE

1 pound venisonburger
1/2 pound venison or bulk Italian pork sausage
1/2 cup onions, chopped
1 teaspoon seasoned salt
1 teaspoon oregano
1/2 teaspoon flaked red pepper
1/2 teaspoon black pepper
1/2 cup barbecue sauce

1/2 teaspoon soy sauce
1 teaspoon red wine
1 teaspoon Worcestershire sauce
14-16 oz. mild salsa
12 oz. tomato puree
2 cups water
4 oz. fresh sliced mushrooms
2 fresh tomatoes, diced

In Dutch oven brown venison and sausage for 15 minutes or so; then add onion, brown until clear. Add salt, oregano, red and black pepper, barbecue sauce, soy sauce, red wine and Worcestershire sauce. Simmer 15-20 minutes. Add salsa and tomato puree to Dutch oven with a cup of water. Stir and simmer 15 minutes. Then add remaining cup of water, sliced mushrooms and diced tomatoes. Stir and cover. Simmer 60 to 90 minutes stirring occasionally. Serve over pasta or cool and freeze for delicious venison pasta any time.

Tom's Festive Venison Lasagna

1/4 of a (1-pound) pkg.
  Lasagna noodles, uncooked
1 lb. bulk venison sausage
1 medium onion, chopped
2 cloves garlic, minced
1 (15 oz.) can whole tomatoes,
  cut up (undrained)
1 (6 oz.) can tomato paste
1 teaspoon sugar
2 teaspoons salt
1/2 teaspoon basil leaves
1/2 teaspoon oregano

1/2 teaspoon crushed red
  pepper
1/4 teaspoon black pepper
1 (15 oz.) container ricotta
  cheese
1 egg, beaten
1/4 cup chopped fresh parsley
1 teaspoon salt
2 cups shredded mozzarella
  cheese
1/2 cup grated Parmesan
  cheese

Prepare Lasagna according to package directions; drain. In Dutch oven, combine sausage, onion and garlic. Cook until sausage is no longer pink, stirring occasionally. Stir in next eight ingredients. Bring to boil. Reduce heat; simmer 20 minutes. In medium bowl, blend ricotta, egg, parsley and salt. Spread a thin layer of sauce in 13 x 9-inch baking pan. Layer one-third each lasagna, remaining sauce, ricotta mixture, mozzarella and Parmesan cheeses. Repeat layers. Bake in a 375 degree oven until bubbly, about 1 hour. Let stand 5 minutes before cutting. 6 servings.

FOOD FOR THOUGHT

VENISON OVEN AND CHARCOAL BROILING GUIDELINES

Cuts	Thickness	Total Approximate Broiling Time
Round Steaks	1¼ inches	15 minutes (rare)
Sirloin Steaks	1¼ inches	18 minutes (medium)
Loin steaks	1¼ inches	20 minutes (well done)

*Always spray your broiler pan with non-stick cooking spray. It helps a lot!

VENISON STEAKS FOR CHARCOAL BROILING

Steaks cut 1 inch thick or more are ideal for charcoal broiling. The cooking time may vary a little depending on the grilling equipment and the fire builder. A guide you can follow is to allow 6-8 minutes per side for 1 inch thick steaks to cook to medium doneness. Steaks or marinated venison roast cut 2 inches thick I suggest you grill the venison slowly over a low charcoal fire so it will brown and not char. A venison steak cut this thick will take 35-40 minutes on each side to cook to medium doneness. Venison tastes best medium rare to medium.

COOKING VENISON TRADITIONAL-STYLE

*V*enison steaks or roasts, whether oven broiled, charcoal grilled or pan fried are best enjoyed medium rare; pink and juicy in the middle. If you want to eat your venison steaks or roasts medium well to well done like you do your beef, then be sure to keep the venison moist during cooking and after because venison is very lean. It can be over cooked and will dry out and be tough. That is one of the most frequent venison cooking mistakes.

Our collection of traditional style recipes have been carefully tested and written to help you easily prepare quality venison for your family's dinner table year after year. We know we are thankful for and proudly prepare every venison meal with our quality cared for venison from field to freezer and then to our dinner table.

T hanks to Bob Mitchell for contributing this recipe. Bob said it was originally his mothers recipe and she used beef. If it was good soup using beef then it would only taste better with Bob's venison he thought. Bob said it is very good because it seems even the most finicky game eaters like it.

MOM'S HEARTY VENISON & MUSHROOM SOUP

1 cup cooked rice
3-4 garlic cloves, minced
1/4 cup olive oil
2 pounds venison roast or stew meat cut in 1/2 inch cubes
1 cup onions, chopped
2 (14 1/2 oz.) cans beef broth

2 cups tomatoes, diced
3/4 cup carrots, chopped
1/2 cup Burgundy wine
1/2 teaspoon salt
1 1/2 teaspoon oregano
1 bay leaf
1 pound mushrooms, sliced
3 strands saffron, optional

Cook rice according to package directions and set aside. In your Dutch oven sauté garlic in half the olive oil. Add cubed venison, onions and remaining olive oil and brown 15-20 minutes, stirring occasionally. Add broth, tomatoes, carrots, and wine; stir and add salt, oregano, and bay leaf. Bring to a boil. Reduce heat and simmer 45-50 minutes so venison and carrots are tender. Add mushrooms, saffron if using, and cooked rice; stir. Over medium heat cook for 10-15 minutes to heat through. Delicious and good for you, too. . .

—*Bob Mitchell, Editor, PA Game News*

Venison Macaroni Supper

An easy, tasty dish for young hunters to prepare!

8 oz. mostaccioll or large macaroni, uncooked

1 pound ground venison

1 cup chopped onion

1 teaspoon salt

16 oz. bag frozen sweet corn

1 can (14½ oz.) stewed tomatoes

½ cup catsup or salsa

Cook pasta using package directions. In a large skillet brown venison with onion and salt. Stir in corn, stewed tomatoes and catsup or salsa; simmer 5 minutes. Stir in macaroni; simmer 5 minutes more.

Deep Lake Venison Steak

1 pound venison loin, 2 inch thick

1 teaspoon garlic powder

1 medium onion, cut in chunks

½ green pepper, cut in strips

½ teaspoon thyme, crushed

2 tablespoons olive oil

1 can (14½ oz.) stewed tomatoes

2 teaspoons cornstarch

Sprinkle venison with ¼ teaspoon garlic powder. Broil 5 inches from heat, 12 to 15 minutes for medium rare, or until cooked as desired, turning once. In skillet, cook onion, green pepper, thyme, and remaining garlic powder in oil until vegetables are tender-crisp. Drain tomatoes reserving juice; combine juice and cornstarch to a cup and blend. Add stewed tomatoes and corn starch to vegetables; cook, stirring constantly, until thickened. Salt and pepper to taste. Thinly slice venison; top with vegetables. Add a baked potato and enjoy!

ROG'S SKILLET VENISON WITH CORN

1 pound venison steak, thinly
   sliced
1 medium onion, chopped
1/2 teaspoon thyme, crushed
1 tablespoon olive oil
1/2 cup red wine
1/2 teaspoon black pepper

1/2 cup catsup
1 can (14 1/2 oz.) stewed
   tomatoes
16 oz. frozen whole kernel
   sweet corn
1 cup cooked rice

In skillet, brown venison, onion and thyme in oil. Stir in wine, black pepper, and catsup; bring to boil. Simmer, uncovered, over medium heat, about 10 minutes or until liquid is gone. Add tomatoes; reduce heat. Cover and cook 20-30 minutes or until venison is tender. Uncover and cook 5 minutes more. Add corn and cooked rice; heat through 10-15 minutes until tender.

*T*hanks to Gale's mom for sharing her beef roast recipe with us. We did not have to change a thing when we tried it on our venison. Delicious! You will want to try it soon even if you only have a 1 1/2 pound venison roast.

MOM'S ROAST OF VENISON

2 to 3 pounds venison roast
2 tablespoons olive oil
1 large onion, sliced
1 jar (16 oz.) salsa
1/2 teaspoon garlic powder

1 (14 1/2 oz.) can beef broth
1 jar (4 oz.) mushrooms
1/2 teaspoon red pepper flakes
1 tablespoon parsley
3 tablespoons flour

In Dutch oven or heavy pot, brown venison in oil. Add onion; cook until soft. Add remaining ingredients, except flour. Cover and simmer 2 to 3 hours or until venison is tender, turning meat occasionally. Remove venison to serving platter; cover to keep warm. To make gravy, dissolve flour in 1/4 cup water. Add 2 tablespoons hot cooking liquid and blend well; add to remaining cooking liquid. Cook, stirring constantly, until thickened. Season to taste with salt and pepper, if desired. Serve sliced venison with mashed potatoes and gravy. Enjoy!

A HUNTER'S VENISON & VEGETABLE SOUP

1 pound ground
  venisonburger
3/4 cup chopped onion
2 cans (14 1/2 oz. ea.) Italian
  style stewed tomatoes
2 cans beef broth

1 pound frozen mixed
  vegetables
1/2 cup uncooked medium
  egg noodles
1/2 teaspoon oregano
1/2 teaspoon parsley
1/2 teaspoon garlic powder

In large pot, brown venison with onion in a little melted butter or olive oil. Cook until onion is tender. Salt and pepper to taste, if desired. Stir in remaining ingredients. Bring to boil; reduce heat. Cover and simmer 30 minutes. Ah, nutritiously delicious!

TASTY VENISON VEGETABLE SOUP

1 pound venison sausage or
  venisonburger
2 (14 1/2 oz.) cans beef broth
1 cup small pasta (uncooked)
1/3 cup favorite steak sauce

1/2 teaspoon each salt and
  black pepper
16 oz. can tomato sauce
10 oz. pkg. frozen mixed
  vegetables

In a large Dutch oven brown venison in 1 tablespoon olive oil for 10 minutes or so. Combine remaining ingredients and bring to a boil. Cover and reduce heat to simmering for 30 minutes. A healthy meal choice, for sure.

This easy and tasty recipe takes about an hour to prepare, but it is worth the effort. The venison zucchini boats can be cut into small pieces for serving as a "special hot appetizer" or served whole with a baked Idaho or sweet potato for an unusual entree.

*F*or a special venison dinner for family or friends you will want to prepare this recipe. Just add your favorite rice and vegetable for a memorable meal occasion.

YUMMY VENISON KEBABS

2¹/₂ to 3 pound venison steak, cut 1 inch thick

¹/₂ pound sliced bacon

8 oz. large, whole fresh mushrooms

2 large green peppers, cut into squares

1 pint container cherry tomatoes

1 stick (¹/₂ cup) butter, softened

1 tablespoon chili powder

2 tablespoons prepared mustard

2 tablespoons Worcestershire sauce

2 tablespoons soy sauce

¹/₂ teaspoon ground black pepper

Cut venison steak into 1¹/₂ inch squares. Wrap a half slice of bacon around each piece of meat. Thread alternating pieces of venison and mushrooms onto 4 skewers, leaving about ¹/₂ inch of space around each piece of venison so bacon will cook evenly. Thread alternating pieces of green pepper and cherry tomatoes onto 4 separate skewers. Blend together remaining ingredients. Spread on venison and vegetables. Place meat and mushroom kebabs on broiler rack in pan and broil 3 inches from heat for about 4 to 5 minutes. Turn. Place green pepper and tomato kebabs on rack with meat. Spread venison and vegetable kebabs with more of the seasoned spread. Broil another 3 to 4 minutes and do not over cook. Juicy medium rare!

CREAMY VENISON BEAN CASSEROLE

1 pound ground
   venisonburger or sausage
1/4 teaspoon pepper
1 pkg. (10 oz.) frozen cut
   green beans
1 can (10³/4 oz.) condensed
   cream of broccoli soup

1/2 teaspoon salt
1/4 cup steak sauce
1 pkg. (10 oz.) frozen lima
   beans
1/2 cup milk
1 can (3 oz.) French fried
   onions

In large skillet, brown venison until crumbly. Mix in remaining ingredients. Pour into greased 10 x 6 x 2 inch baking dish. Bake in preheated 350 degree oven 20 minutes or until bubbly. Top with onion rings. Continue baking 5 minutes or until onions are crisp.

VENISON PAN-BROILED WITH MUSTARD SAUCE

1 pound venison loin steaks, cut 1/2 to 3/4 inch thick

MUSTARD SAUCE INGREDIENTS:

3 tablespoons prepared
   mustard
3-4 drops Tabasco sauce
1 tablespoon vinegar

2 tablespoons butter
1/2 teaspoon garlic salt
1 teaspoon black pepper

Rub skillet with butter. Brown venison steaks over medium to high heat. Turn to cook and brown evenly, about 8 to 12 minutes for medium-done steaks. Mix remaining ingredients to a smooth paste. Five minutes before steaks are done, top with mustard sauce and simmer 2 minutes more.

Cooking Tip: Do not cook too long. Venison is juicy and delicious medium rare to medium (pink in middle) like the best beef.

VENISON STUFFED ZUCCHINI BOATS
(Serves Six)

3 pounds zucchini
1 pound ground venison
3 tablespoons steak sauce
1/4 cup chopped onion
1 clove garlic, minced

1 teaspoon black pepper
1 jar (16 oz.) spaghetti sauce
1 cup (4 oz.) shredded mild cheddar cheese
1/2 cup dry bread crumbs

In boiling salted water, cook zucchini 3 minutes. Drain. Cut in half lengthwise. Scoop out seeds to form shell. Set aside and use zucchini later as a vegetable side dish. In large skillet, brown venison until crumbly. Mix in steak sauce, onion, garlic, black pepper, spaghetti sauce and 1/2 cheese. Preheat oven to 350 degrees. Fill zucchini boats with venison mixture. Arrange in 13 x 9 x 2 inch baking pan. Combine bread crumbs with remaining cheese. Sprinkle on top. Bake in preheated 350 degree oven 35 minutes. Deliciously nutritious.

GALE'S CHUNKY VENISON & MUSHROOM CHILI

2 tablespoons olive oil
1 pound venison steak, cut in one inch cubes
1 cup chopped green onions
4 teaspoons chili powder
1 1/2 teaspoons ground cumin
3 cloves garlic, minced
1 teaspoon black pepper

1 teaspoon cayenne pepper (optional)
1 pound fresh white mushrooms, quartered
2 (14 1/2 oz.) cans crushed tomatoes
3 (14 1/2 oz.) cans red kidney beans, or chili beans
1 teaspoon salt

In a Dutch oven or large sauce pan heat oil until hot. Add venison, cook, stirring occasionally, until brown, about 10 to 15 minutes. Add onion; cook, stirring frequently. Stir in chili powder, cumin, garlic, black and cayenne pepper; cook, stirring frequently, about 10 minutes. Add mushrooms, tomatoes, beans and salt; bring to a boil. Reduce heat and simmer covered about 30-40 minutes. Serve with grated cheese, hot sauce, and garlic bread or biscuits.

This tasty dish is easy to prepare and is delicious over noodles, rice or even potatoes of your choice.

QUICK CURRIED VENISON & TOMATOES

Young hunters should especially cook this dish. They will be proud of how good it tastes, and they will be proud of the complements.

½ stick (¼ cup) butter	6 ounce can tomato paste
1½ pounds venison stew meat, cut into 1 inch cubes	2 teaspoons soy sauce
1 medium onion, chopped	1½ teaspoons curry powder
2 teaspoons sugar	¼ teaspoon black pepper
½ teaspoon salt	1 pound can cooked tomatoes
1 teaspoon garlic powder	2 tablespoons lemon juice
	½ cup hot water

Melt butter in Dutch oven. Brown venison on all sides 10-15 minutes; add onion and cook with venison until transparent. Add remaining ingredients and stir well to combine. Simmer about 1 hour 30 minutes, or until venison is tender.

 A DEER HUNTER'S WIFE KNOWS!
It is not hard to see how your man, over time, sees deer hunting as a tradition that is really looked forward to. He always saves the vacation time needed, hunts the same woods, large or small, with the same family members or "hunting buddies." And very important is the fact that they will usually share their venison if someone does not take their deer, even if it was because of a missed shot.

*V*enison prepared as easily as this is always
delicious and nutritious, too! When we had this
venison meal we added baked sweet potatoes and
frozen peas with fresh mushrooms. A nice family
meal with rice of your choice also.

So Good ... Venison & Veggies

1 envelope of savory herb
  with garlic or Italian herb
  with tomato soup mix

2 pounds venison roast or
  stew meat, cubed

1 onion, chopped

1 pound potatoes, sliced thin

2 large carrots, sliced thin

2 stalks celery, sliced thin

2 cups water

1 cup mushrooms, sliced

Preheat oven to 350 degrees. To a regular size cooking bag add 2 tablespoons flour; seal and shake to coat. Place in a 9 x 13 inch baking dish. To bag add one envelope of soup, cubed venison, onions, potatoes, carrots and celery. Hold bag at top and toss to mix ingredients and place in dish. Open bag and add water and mushrooms. Tie off the bag and poke 6-8 holes in top of bag. Roast for 1-1/2 hours; then remove dinner from oven. Let stand 15-20 minutes to cool. Open bag and pour the delicious smelling meal into baking dish to serve. AH, Enjoy!

STEVE'S VENISON ROUND STEAK

1/3 cup butter
1/4 cup flour
2 teaspoons salt
1/2 teaspoon black pepper
2 to 2 1/2 pounds venison
  round steak, 1 inch thick
1 cup beef bouillon

3 carrots, pared and sliced
  diagonally
2 medium onions, sliced and
  separated into rings
1 teaspoon chili powder
1 cup dairy sour cream

Melt butter in a Dutch oven. Combine flour, salt, and black pepper, reserving 2 tablespoons of the seasoned flour. Dip venison into seasoned flour. Brown venison slowly on each side in melted butter. Add beef bouillon, cover and simmer 1 hour. Remove lid and add carrots and onions. Simmer an additional 20 to 30 minutes, or until carrots are tender. Remove venison and vegetables to a hot platter and cover. Stir chili powder into sour cream in Dutch oven. Gradually blend in 2 tablespoons of seasoned flour to meat juices and heat slowly for 5 minutes. To serve, spoon gravy and vegetables over venison and serve hot with mashed potatoes or baked sweet potatoes .. AH! So, So Tasty!

VENISON POT ROAST CHINESE

4 to 5 pound venison roast
1/2 cup butter
1/2 cup water
1 cup finely chopped green
  pepper
1 cup chopped celery

4 ounce can button
  mushrooms with liquid
1 cup finely chopped onion
1 teaspoon ginger
3 tablespoons soy sauce
1 teaspoon parsley

Place venison roast in Dutch oven and brown in butter on all sides. In a small bowl mix remaining ingredients and add to roast. Cover tightly and cook slowly on top of the range or in a moderate oven (350 degrees) about 2 1/2 hours, or until fork tender. Remove roast and keep hot. Remove vegetables with slotted spoon. Measure liquid and add water to bring total to 2 cups. Stir in 2 tablespoons cornstarch mixed with a little cold water. Cook and stir until thickened. Add vegetables and serve hot with venison roast. AH!

9-POINT VENISON STEAK ROYAL

2 pounds venison round
  steak, cut into 1 inch pieces
3 tablespoons olive oil
1 cup chopped onion
1/3 cup chopped green pepper
4 ounce can sliced
  mushrooms and liquid
8 ounce can tomato sauce
1 cup water

1 teaspoon salt
1/4 teaspoon black pepper
1/2 teaspoon oregano
1/3 cup water
2 tablespoons flour
1 1/2 cups dairy sour cream
Hot cooked noodles or baked
  potatoes

In a fry pan, brown venison in olive oil 15 to 20 minutes. Add onion, green pepper, mushrooms and liquid, tomato sauce, 1 cup water, salt, black pepper, and oregano. Cover and simmer for 1 hour or until venison is tender. Combine 1/3 cup water and flour and mix until smooth. Add to liquid in skillet and stir and cook until gravy is thickened. Gradually stir in sour cream and simmer 5 minutes. Serve over noodles or baked potatoes.

AN OLD-FASHIONED VENISON STEW

2 pounds venison stew meat,
  1 inch cubes
1/3 cup flour
2 tablespoons butter
1 1/2 to 2 teaspoons salt
1/2 teaspoon dried leaf thyme
1 teaspoon chili powder
1/2 teaspoon black pepper

2 1/2 cups water
2 tablespoons salsa or catsup
6 medium potatoes, pared and
  cut into 1 inch cubes
1 bunch green onions,
  chopped
6 medium carrots, pared and
  cut into 1 inch pieces

Roll venison cubes in flour to coat all sides. Use all the flour. Brown it in butter in large skillet with a lid or Dutch oven. Sprinkle salt, thyme, chili powder, and black pepper over the venison. Add water and salsa or catsup. Cover with tight-fitting lid, and cook slowly over low heat 45 minutes. Stir in vegetables. Cover and continue cooking 30 minutes, or until vegetables are just done. Pass the bread and red wine for me, please!

You will find this spicy venison dish hearty and nutritious, easy to prepare and even easier to eat at home or camp. I first had this tasty venison dish before deer hunting with Rick, a long time friend of mine, years back. After our meal, Sue, Rick's wife, gave me her recipe that we enjoy at least yearly ever since.
Thanks Sue and Rick!

RICK'S DEER TRAIL VENISON

2 tablespoons olive oil

1 large onion, diced

1 pound mild or hot Italian sausage links, sliced thin

2¹/₂ teaspoons chili powder

2 teaspoons garlic powder

1 teaspoon Italian seasoning

1 teaspoon oregano

¹/₂ to 1 teaspoon red pepper flakes (optional)

1¹/₂ to 2 pounds boneless venison shoulder or stew meat, cut into 1 inch cubes

1 (14 oz.) can beef broth

2 cups stewed tomatoes

¹/₂ cup tomato paste

1 can green chili peppers

1 teaspoon brown sugar

1 cup mushrooms sliced

1 bell pepper, chopped

1 teaspoon salt

¹/₂ teaspoon black pepper

2 teaspoons parsley

Put 2 tablespoons oil in your Dutch oven. Add onion and cook for 10 minutes or so, stirring occasionally. Add sliced sausage into the Dutch oven and brown over medium heat for 10 minutes. Stir occasionally and add chili, garlic powder, Italian seasoning, oregano, and pepper flakes. Stir and add cubed venison and cook 15 minutes or so. Then add beef broth, stewed tomatoes, tomato paste, chili peppers, and brown sugar. Simmer covered on low heat for 45 minutes, stirring occasionally. Add mushrooms, bell pepper, salt, black pepper, and parsley; stir to bend and continue simmering for additional 45 minutes or until venison is tender. Serve this hearty venison dish over rice or noodles. As always, enjoy!

Deer Heart — Pink's Style

*Special thanks to our friend and Pennsylvania
Outdoor Writer's Association member, Charlie Burchfield
for contributing a recipe favorite of his called
"Deer Heart — Pink's Style". We will sample this recipe
just as soon as we can — so Pennsylvania and the
rest of the country, give it a try. This is a special dish at
Paradise Ranch in Julian, Pennsylvania.*

Venison cuts are enjoyed in may ways however; there is one piece of meat that is often disregarded as table fare and that is the heart. Deer heart can be prepared at camp shortly after the deer has been taken or cleaned and frozen for use later. Regardless of your choice, here is a recipe that is quick, simple and sure to tantalize the taste buds.

Take one deer heart. Remove connecting arteries, then flush and clean with cold water. The meat can be soaked in a solution of salt water for several hours to help draw any excess blood from the cavities of the meat.

To prepare for cooking, slice the heart in half lengthwise then the halves are to be cut into strips. Place the strips into a plastic bag and add the liquid from a jar of Pink's Peppers. Hold the peppers for later use. Pink's Peppers is a blend of Hungarian wax peppers along with a number of other spices that offer a unique flavor. Pink's Peppers are available in regular and hot.

Allow the meat to marinate for two or three hours. To prepare, place the meat in a medium hot frying pan along with enough of the marinade to cover the bottom of the pan. Allow the meat to cook four or five minutes. Next add the drained peppers. Additional marinade can be added if needed to keep the peppers from drying out before they are completely cooked. Marinade can be added as needed to provide moisture while cooking.

To add zip to the flavor of this dish, cook the liquid down while browning the meat. Then add the drained peppers and cook the mix until the peppers become soft. Be careful not to allow the meat or peppers to burn. Again, add marinade as needed.

The dish makes a great appetizer. And can be served together with fresh Italian bread. And if you don't tell them, they'll never know what they are eating and more than likely ask for more.

STEVE'S DEER CAMP VENISON GOULASH
An Easy Dish to Serve 4

1 pound venison stew meat, cubed
3-4 teaspoons flour
1 cup onions, chopped
2 garlic cloves, diced
1/2 teaspoon salt
1 teaspoon black pepper

2 (14-16 oz.) cans stewed tomatoes
1 (14-1/2 oz.) can beef broth
1 cup catsup or salsa
2 (14-16 oz.) cans whole potatoes, drained and cubed
1 can mixed vegetables

Combine venison and flour in a bag, toss to coat. Brown venison in 2 tablespoons of butter or olive oil in a Dutch oven. Add onions and garlic; cook 5 minutes or until tender, and add salt and pepper. Add tomatoes, broth, and catsup or salsa and bring to a boil. Reduce heat and simmer, covered, 45-60 minutes or until the venison is tender. Add potatoes and mixed vegetables. Then cook uncovered 5-10 minutes. Add hot sauce to taste to get rid of the winter chill. Pass the bread please .... Enjoy!

Tip: This venison dish prepares in half the time if you substitute venisonburger or venison sausage.

RICK'S QUICK VENISON ITALIANO

1 teaspoon garlic, diced
2 tablespoons all-purpose flour
1/4 teaspoon black pepper
1/2 Italian seasoning

1/2 teaspoon salt
1 pound venison steak, cut into small chunks
2 tablespoons olive oil
1 (16 oz.) can stewed tomatoes

Mix garlic, flour, pepper, Italian seasoning, and salt on plate. Coat venison completely; shake off excess. In large skillet over medium-high heat, heat olive oil. Cook venison 10 minutes or until browned on all sides. Add stewed tomatoes; stir to combine. Heat to a boil. Cover and cook over low heat 20-30 minutes or until venison is tender. Serve over rice! AH ....

*T*his is a favorite, easy and tasty venison meal to prepare. We used rice but if you prefer, one pound sliced potatoes can be substituted. Hot spice can be added individually after serving this tasty venison dish. Serves 4.

DAD'S BARBECUE STYLE VENISON ROAST

1/4 cup flour
1 Reynolds cooking bag
2 garlic cloves, diced
1 cup chopped onion
2 stalks celery
2 carrots
2 pounds venison roast, cubed

1 cup barbecue sauce
1 teaspoon salt
1 teaspoon chili powder
1 teaspoon Italian seasoning
1 cup of rice, adding enough water to cook according to pkg. directions
1 cup water

Preheat oven to 325 degrees. Shake up flour in your Reynolds cooking bag and place in a 13 x 9 x 2 inch baking pan. Add garlic, onion, celery, carrots and venison. Seal bag and toss to mix. Add barbecue sauce, salt, chili powder, Italian seasoning, rice and water mixture, plus the 1 cup water. Close bag with nylon tie; make 5-6 small slits in top of bag. Bake for 1 1/2 hours.

Remove from oven and let this dish cool 15-20 minutes before opening bag to serve. Enjoy!

You know I am still proud that I have been a part of Steve's traditional deer hunting for twenty-six plus years and I cannot recall a single time when he talked about how it felt to kill his deer. He talks about the events of how he took the deer and finishes with thanksgiving to the Lord for the nutritious, delicious venison the deer will again provide for our family's dinner table.

—Gale Loder

*H*ere *is another easy yet tasty treat you will need to try.*
AH!

Souperburger Sloppy Joes

2 tablespoons butter
1 pound ground venison
1 cup onion, chopped
1/2 teaspoon garlic, diced
1 (10³/4 oz.) can condensed
  golden mushroom soup

2 tablespoons prepared
  mustard
1/2 teaspoon black pepper
6 hamburger rolls, split and
  toasted

Melt butter in large skillet, add venison, onion, and garlic, and cook over medium-high heat until the venison is browned, stirring to separate meat. Stir in soup, mustard, and black pepper. Simmer over low heat until heated through. Pour meat mixture over rolls, and serve with a favorite vegetable.

Dad's Venison Meat Loaf

Thanks, Dad, for an easy and tasty meal ....

1 (10³/4 oz.) can condensed
  golden mushroom soup,
  *divided
2 pounds venisonburger
1 pouch dry onion soup and
  recipe mix
1/2 cup dry bread crumbs

1 egg, beaten
1/4 cup catsup
1 teaspoon prepared mustard
1 teaspoon Italian seasoning
1/4 cup water

In large bowl thoroughly mix 1/2 can mushroom soup, venisonburger, onion soup mix, bread crumbs, egg, catsup, mustard, and Italian seasoning. In baking pan shape mixture firmly into 8 x 4 inch loaf. Bake at 350 degrees for 1¹/2 hours or until meat loaf is done. In small saucepan mix 2 tablespoons drippings, remaining 1/2 can mushroom soup and water. Heat through. Serve with meat loaf as a gravy. Great with baked potatoes or baked French fries. ENJOY!

ELLA'S VENISON & VEGETABLE SOUP

*Thanks for contributing one of your deer
hunter recipes, Ella!*

2 pounds venison stew meat
   or shank and hocks (4), cut
   into 1 inch cubes
4 tablespoons butter
8 cups cold water
2 bay leaves
1/2 teaspoon ground
   marjoram
1 teaspoon oregano
1 tablespoon salt
1/2 teaspoon ground thyme

1 teaspoon parsley
1/2 teaspoon pepper
1 1/2 teaspoons salt
1 medium onion, sliced
1/2 cup celery, sliced
1/2 cup uncooked rice
1 (10 oz.) pkg. frozen lima
   beans
1 (10 oz.) pkg. frozen corn
1 cup carrots, sliced
1 pound can stewed tomatoes

In a Dutch oven add venison and brown well on all sides in butter.
Add cold water and remaining seasonings, onion, and celery; stir.
Heat gradually to the boiling point, cover and simmer for 2 hours.
Then add rice, lima beans, corn, carrots, and tomatoes and simmer
for 45 minutes. Delicious ...

QUICK VENISON SAUSAGE WITH RED BEANS & RICE

4 cups cooked rice
1 pound venison sausage
2 (16 oz.) cans chili or kidney
   beans
1 cup catsup
2 tablespoons salsa (med.
   hot) (optional)

1 tablespoon chili powder
1 large onion, peeled and
   chopped
2 cloves garlic, diced
2 teaspoons Worcestershire
   sauce

Cook rice according to package directions, and set aside. In large
Dutch oven over low heat, sauté sausage until lightly browned.
Combine remaining ingredients, except rice and stir. Cover and
simmer 30-40 minutes. Serve over cooked rice. For 4-6 people.
Easy and tasty dish!

GALE'S HOLIDAY ROAST OF VENISON

Guaranteed you will enjoy this savory dish. Just ask my brother and his wife.

1/3 cup flour
1 large size Reynolds oven bag
3 garlic cloves, diced
1 teaspoon chili powder
1 (16 oz.) jar salsa or chili sauce (sweet)

1 (15-16 oz.) can stewed tomatoes
2 carrots, chopped
1 cup onion, chopped
1 green pepper, cut in strips
2 to 2 1/2 pounds boneless venison shoulder

Preheat oven to 325 degrees. Shake flour in oven bag and place in a 13 x 9 x 2 inch baking dish. Then add garlic, chili powder, salsa or chili sauce, tomatoes, carrots, onion, and green pepper; squeeze bag to blend ingredients before adding your venison. Now squeeze bag again to mix well. Close bag with nylon tie; cut 6 holes in top. Bake 1 1/2 hours. Remove your holiday roast from oven and let it cool 10 minutes before removing to serve. Serve with baked potatoes and a glass of your favorite merlot or classic burgundy wine.

VENISON ROAST WITH SOUR CREAM GRAVY

3 to 4 pound venison roast
1/2 cup olive oil
2 medium onions, thinly sliced
8 ounce can water chestnuts, sliced or fresh mushrooms

1 tablespoon salt
1 1/2 teaspoons parsley
1 teaspoon Italian seasoning
1 cup water
2 tablespoons flour
1 cup dairy sour cream

In Dutch oven brown venison roast on all sides in olive oil. Add onions, water chestnuts or mushrooms, salt, parsley, Italian seasoning, and water. Cover and cook slowly on top of the stove or in a moderate oven (350 degrees) about 2 1/2 hours, or until venison is fork tender. Remove roast. Mix flour into sour cream and gradually stir into pan drippings, stirring until thickened. Serve gravy over slices of venison and mashed potatoes. Enjoy!

*T*his sauce tastefully complimented our venison steak rather than overpowering it. It was a delightful entree that went exceptionally well with sweet potatoes and a glass of our favorite Merlot.

VENISON STEAKS IN DEER HUNTER'S SAUCE

2 pounds venison steaks

PREPARE YOUR DEER HUNTERS SAUCE:

2 tablespoons butter
1 cup onions, chopped
2-3 garlic cloves, diced
1/2 cup tomato juice or salsa
4 oz. jar green chili peppers

1 teaspoon salt
1/2 teaspoon black or hot pepper
1 tablespoon parsley
1/2 teaspoon chili powder

Melt butter in skillet and sauté onions, and garlic 5 minutes. Then add remaining ingredients and simmer 15-20 minutes, stirring occasionally. While sauce is cooking preheat oven to 350 degrees. When sauce is done pour half into a 9 x 13 baking dish and add venison steaks. Top steaks with remaining deer hunters sauce. Bake uncovered for 45-60 minutes depending on doneness preference. Venison is served at its juicy best medium rare to medium.

SPICY PAN-BROILED VENISON STEAKS

1 1/2 to 2 pounds venison round steaks, cut 1/2 inch to 3/4 inch thick
1 stick (1/2 cup) butter
1 teaspoon garlic salt

1 teaspoons salt
2 teaspoons chili powder
1 tablespoon paprika
1/2 teaspoon black pepper

Brown steaks in butter over medium to high heat. Turn to cook and brown evenly, about 10 to 15 minutes for medium done steaks. Do not add water or a cover. In a cup mix together remaining ingredients. Five minutes before steaks are done, spread lightly with the spicy seasonings mixture. Serve hot with baked Idaho or sweet potatoes.

*H*ere *is just the venison steak appetizer you have been looking for to enjoy any time. Next time you prepare it you will likely double it so there are some leftovers ....*

BUCK STEAK APPETIZER WITH DIP OF YOUR CHOICE

1 pound venison steak,   **Rye bread**
  cut 1 inch to 1 1/2 inch thick

Place steak on broiler rack in pan so that top of steak is 3 to 4 inches from the heat. Broil until one side is brown, or 10 minutes. Turn. Broil other side. A 1 1/4 inch thick steak will be medium done in about 20 minutes. Medium rare to medium doneness is best. Be careful not to overcook. Place steak on cutting board and slice into strips about 1/2 inch wide and 2 inch long. Serve on small round slices of rye bread. Top with one of the two following sauces: (Option: Fry venison steak in butter until medium doneness.)

SOUR CREAM-HORSERADISH SAUCE

1 tablespoon butter   **2 to 3 tablespoons hot**
1 tablespoon flour   **horseradish**
1/4 teaspoon salt   **1 cup dairy sour cream**
1/4 teaspoon sugar   **1 teaspoon lemon juice**
1/4 cup milk   **1 teaspoon garlic powder**
                                     1 teaspoon parsley

Melt butter in a saucepan. Blend in flour, salt, and sugar. Add milk and horseradish. Stir and cook until mixture becomes quite thick. Gradually stir in sour cream. Add lemon juice, garlic powder, and parsley. Heat slowly; do not boil. Serve hot or chilled on venison and rye bread.

SOUR CREAM DIP

1 cup dairy sour cream   **1/4 teaspoon salt**
2 tablespoons chopped green   **1/2 teaspoon garlic powder**
  onion tops

Combine all ingredients. Chill before serving on venison and rye bread.

*M*ake this steak for your wife and she'll hug your
neck. Guaranteed, the next time you prepare
this recipe you will double it so you can have
seconds or at least delicious leftovers.

VENISON STEAK HONG KONG

6 tablespoons soy sauce
2 tablespoons sugar
2 cloves garlic, crushed

1/4 to 1/2 teaspoon ground
ginger
1 pound venison loin

Combine soy sauce, sugar, garlic, and ginger in a pan. Marinate
venison in this sauce for several hours in the refrigerator. Place
venison on broiler rack in pan so tops of venison steaks are 3 to 4
inches from heat. Broil until one side is brown. Turn. Broil other
side. A 1 1/4 inch steak will be medium done in about 20 minutes
total cooking time. Pour remaining marinade into steak drippings
in broiler pan. Heat and pour over venison steaks. Serve hot with a
baked potato and a favorite vegetable. Yields two servings.

OLÉ BUCK STEAKS WITH TOMATO SAUCE MARINADE

8 ounce can tomato sauce
1 tablespoon soy sauce
2 cloves garlic, crushed

1/2 teaspoon Italian seasoning
1/2 teaspoon parsley
1 to 1 1/2 pounds venison loin
steaks

Combine tomato sauce, soy sauce, crushed garlic, Italian seasoning, and parsley in a glass baking dish; add steaks and cover. Marinate steaks in this sauce in the refrigerator about 2 1/2 hours, turning steaks occasionally. Place steaks on broiler rack in pan so tops
of steaks are 3 to 4 inches from heat. Broil until one side is brown.
Turn. Broil other side. A 1 1/4 inch thick steak will be medium done
in abut 20 minutes total cooking time. While your steaks are cooking add marinade to small pan and cook 10 minutes. When your
steaks are done, place them on a serving platter and pour over the
tomato sauce marinade. Yup - so, so good . . . You can count on it!!

COOKING
THE LODER FAMILY'S
VENISON FAVORITES

*W*hile *our creativity and our adventuresome taste buds usually mean trying or making up new tasty ways to prepare our quality cared for venison meal after meal each year, we do have our new favorites, too! Now they are here for you to try and enjoy.*

Remember with your deer being properly field dressed and carefully processed you, too, can be creative with recipe ingredients used in preparing your own recipes. Spice them up, down, change them to include your favorite vegetables or wine, for example. Favorite recipes include spices, vegetables, etc. that you and your family especially like, so experiment. You will see great venison cooking is not always in the recipe you use but it always comes from your quality cared for venison that you had to start with. When you have fun cooking, the complements are not far behind. Oh, this is awesome!

While we lived in the deep south we were exposed to Cajun and Creole cooking. We like it but Cajun can be too hot in some dishes. Like chili, venison gumbo is made very hot to mild depending on the hunter's preference. This savory stew makes enough for an army. Freeze leftovers to enjoy gumbo all winter long, adding Tabasco sauce or cayenne pepper to get your hot and spicy flavoring.

*W*e first made this Cajun stew recipe for our church's wild game feast. It was superb like all dishes coming out of our crock pot. When spooned over rice or noodles it makes enough to feed a large family gathering or eight to ten hungry hunters. You can vary the amount of cayenne pepper or Jalapenos to your own taste preferences. Be ready for plenty of compliments. So good!

NEW ORLEANS STYLE VENISON GUMBO

1 pound venison bulk sausage, or store bought Italian Sausage

2 pounds venison stew meat, cubed

1 cup onions, diced

1 cup green onions, chopped

2 cups frozen okra

1 (15 oz.) can tomatoes, crushed

1 (4 oz.) can (mild) green chili peppers or (hot) jalapeno peppers

2 stalks celery, chopped

2-3 garlic cloves, diced

1 teaspoon each Italian seasoning, chives, and basil

1 teaspoon dry mustard

1/4 cup parsley

2 teaspoons chili powder

1 (14 oz.) can beef broth

1 (6 oz.) can shrimp or oysters

1 cup gravy, any kind (optional)

1/4 cup cocktail sauce or chili sauce

2 cans water

1/2 cup bottled clam juice

Brown sausage in a frying pan; drain before adding to your crock pot. In a 6 quart slow cooker add bulk venison sausage, venison stew meat, all remaining ingredients. Cook on high 6-7 hours. Enjoy this Cajun stew over hot rice of your choice. Add cayenne pepper or hot sauce if desired.

You will not go wrong if you prepare this venison loin steak recipe for your very next special occasion. Be careful not to over cook because venison, even more than beef, is at its juicy best and flavorful when served medium rare. (Pink in the middle)

VENISON TENDERLOIN SPECIAL

3 pounds venison loin steaks
3 tablespoons black pepper
1/2 teaspoon garlic salt
1/4 cup olive oil

1 cup dark red wine
1/4 cup bourbon
2 tablespoons spicy mustard
1/4 cup heavy cream

Preheat your oven to 350 degrees. Thaw venison loin steak in refrigerator slowly 1- 2 days before serving. Begin by trimming any remaining silver skin from the loin steaks and press black pepper and garlic salt into both sides of the steaks. In a small bowl prepare your seasoned sauce by mixing olive oil, wine, bourbon, mustard, and heavy cream together. Spray 9 x 13 baking dish with cooking spray and pour in half of the cooking sauce. Place venison steaks in the baking dish and pour remaining cooking sauce over them. Bake at 350 degrees for 40 to 50 minutes. Venison is tender and juicy medium rare. For a memorable meal just add a baked potato and a favorite vegetable. This dish is a family favorite.

STEVE'S EASY VENISON LOIN ROSÉ

1¹/₂ pounds venison loin steak
¹/₂ teaspoon each salt, pepper, Italian seasoning
¹/₄ cup butter or olive oil
1 cup catsup or salsa
¹/₂ cup Rosé wine
¹/₃ cup water
2 tablespoons lemon juice
1 medium onion, minced

1 tablespoon Worcestershire sauce
1 tablespoon soy sauce
1 teaspoon parsley
1 teaspoon thyme
1 cup fresh mushrooms, sliced
¹/₂ teaspoon chili powder

Preheat oven to 325 degrees F. Season both sides of the venison steak with salt, pepper and Italian seasoning. Use your butter or olive oil to brown your steak. When evenly browned, remove and place in 2 quart casserole dish. Combine your remaining ingredients in a sauce pan, bring to a boil and pour ¹/₂ over your venison steak. Turn steak and pour remaining sauce over steak. Bake covered for 40-45 minutes. Enjoy medium rare! Serve with your favorite rice or noodles and hot biscuits or fresh bread. Enjoy!

A FAVORITE VENISON STROGANOFF

¹/₃ cup butter
1 pound venison steak, thinly sliced
1 cup finely chopped green onions
1 cup mushrooms, sliced
10³/₄ oz. can condensed golden mushroom soup
1 cup milk

1 cup sour cream
¹/₂ teaspoon chili powder
¹/₂ teaspoon garlic powder
1 teaspoon salt
¹/₂ teaspoon black pepper
8 oz. bow ties, fettuccine, or your favorite pasta, uncooked

In a large skillet melt butter to brown slices of venison steak with green onions and mushrooms. Blend in soup and milk and simmer 20 to 30 minutes. Stir in sour cream, chili powder, garlic powder, salt and black pepper. Simmer 5 to 10 minutes, being careful not to boil. Serve venison Stroganoff over your favorite pasta prepared as instructed. Enjoy!

*Y*ou've got to try this simple to make, but yet
deliciously nutritious dish as soon as possible. You
will be glad you did. Guaranteed to be so good!

KELLY'S VENISON STEAK WITH FRESH MUSHROOMS

1¹/₂ to 2 pounds venison
steak cut into small bite size
pieces

¹/₃ cup olive oil

1 pound fresh mushrooms,
sliced

8-10 or a bunch of green
onions, chopped

1 green pepper, chopped

2-3 garlic cloves, minced

2 tablespoons flour

1 bouillon cube

1 cup boiling water

1 pound canned stewed
tomatoes

¹/₄ cup Worcestershire sauce

In a large Dutch oven sauté venison in olive oil and set venison
aside. Sauté mushrooms, onion, green pepper and garlic in same
olive oil and stir in flour to thicken. Dissolve bouillon in water and
add it along with tomatoes and Worcestershire sauce to Dutch oven.
Add venison back and stir. Simmer one hour or until your venison
is tender. Serve over rice or noodles.

T his is truly a new favorite recipe of ours to enjoy the best venison steak from the whitetail deer. While easy to prepare it is memorable steak for four special people perhaps celebrating a special event. You have to give this recipe a try. AWESOME! You will see.

PEPPERY VENISON LOIN STEAK

½ cup butter

⅓ cup parsley - fresh is better

⅓ cup minced green or white onions

2 tablespoons Worcestershire sauce

2 tablespoons soy sauce

1 teaspoon black pepper

¼ teaspoon cayenne pepper

1 teaspoon dry mustard

2 pounds of venison back strap (loin) (silver skin removed)

Combine butter, parsley, onion, Worcestershire and soy sauce, peppers and mustard in a small sauce pan. Stir continually while heating over low heat, until butter melts. Reserve ¼ of this sauce. Place the venison loin on the grill or skillet. Brush steak with butter sauce, turn it over and brush the other side. Cook basting frequently with butter sauce until medium rare, about 4-8 minutes a side, depending on the thickness of your loin steaks. Place steak on a platter and cut thin slices across the grain and top with reserved butter sauce. *Be careful not to overcook lean venison steak You want it tender and juicy ....

*W*e *first prepared this recipe over 10 years ago as a holiday appetizer. It was so good with our quality cared for venison that I processed myself, that we use it annually on holiday get togethers. Give this recipe a try soon and see for yourself how tasty venison prepared this way can be.*

PARTY VENISON STEAK TIDBITS

1 to 1¹/₂ pounds venison steaks

¹/₃ cup soy sauce (light, optional)

2 cloves garlic, minced

¹/₂ teaspoon ground ginger

¹/₂ cup Burgundy wine

2 tablespoons brown sugar

¹/₂ teaspoon onion powder

¹/₂ teaspoon chili powder

Place steaks in a 6 x 10 inch glass baking dish. Combine remaining marinade ingredients in small bowl and mix well. Pour over venison to marinate 4 to 5 hours or overnight. Broil venison in the oven 10 to 12 minutes turning once or charcoal grill steaks to medium rare. Heat marinade in small sauce pan to boiling and simmer 5 to 6 minutes. Now serve venison steaks cut into thin strips or small cubes with toothpicks using "hot" marinade as a steak dip. Excellent "hot" appetizer, wow!

 A DEER HUNTER'S WIFE KNOWS!
It does not take long for most families to become dependent on quality cared·for venison from the field to their freezer. That other red meat is not only tasty, but good for you and can easily replace beef around your home as it has in ours. Year after year you are very glad your husband and maybe you, too, deer hunt.

OUR SWEET-SOUR VENISON STEW

1/4 cup flour

1 teaspoon salt

1/2 teaspoon pepper

4 tablespoons butter

2 pounds venison stew meat, cut into 1 1/2 inch cubes

6 large carrots, cut in 3/4 inch pieces

1 cup chopped onion

1 cup fresh mushrooms

2 tablespoons Worcestershire sauce

1/4 cup brown sugar

1/2 cup vinegar

Mix flour, salt and pepper and dredge venison with mixture. Heat butter in skillet and brown venison well. Place carrots in bottom of slow cooker. Add venison, onions, and mushrooms. Combine remaining ingredients and add to cooker. Cook 7 to 8 hours on automatic or 5 to 6 hours on high. Add sweet potatoes and a glass of your favorite Burgundy wine for a savory meal!

A FAVORITE VENISON ROAST MARINADE

1 cup olive oil

1 cup soy sauce

1/2 cup lemon juice

1/3 cup Worcestershire sauce

1/3 cup prepared mustard

10 garlic cloves, cut in half

1 tablespoon black pepper and salt to taste

1/2 teaspoon Cayenne pepper, optional

Pierce venison roast at one inch intervals with a knife and place in a large, heavy duty plastic bag or two. Can use large plastic meat marinader, too. Combine olive oil and next five ingredients. Pour over roast, seal bag and chill 24 to 48 hours. Turn roast occasionally. Remove roast from marinade, discard marinade. Place roast on a lightly greased rack in a broiler pan and sprinkle with black pepper and salt to taste. May add Cayenne pepper at this time. Bake at 325 degrees until done. Meat thermometer should register 145 degrees for medium rare or 160 degrees for medium.

If cooking your venison roast in a smoker, apple wood or hickory adds a great flavor. Smoke for approximately 3 to 5 hours depending on size of your venison roast. Be careful to keep water in your drip pan and do not over cook because venison is very lean and can dry out. Venison is at its very best eaten medium rare.

*W*ell, if you are at deer camp or you are planning a special venison dinner at home for a crowd of family or friends we HAVE to suggest you prepare this special venison dish. Serve with your favorite side dishes of rice, sweet or baked potatoes and a vegetable or two for a truly <u>memorable meal</u>.

STEVE'S SPECIAL ROAST OF VENISON

7 - 9 pound hind quarter of venison, boned with hock and shank removed

1 tablespoon of flour

2 teaspoons salt

1 teaspoon black pepper

1 cup chopped onions

4 garlic cloves, diced

¹/₄ cup lemon juice

1 (14 oz.) can beef broth

1¹/₂ cups good Burgundy wine, *not cooking wine*

Preheat your oven to 350 degrees. Into a large size oven cooking bag put 1 tablespoon of flour and shake. Now place it in a large roasting pan at least 2 inches deep. Open your hind quarter of venison. Season with one teaspoon salt, ¹/₂ teaspoon pepper, ¹/₂ cup chopped onions and ¹/₂ diced garlic. Fold up hind quarter roast and season with remaining salt, black pepper, onions and garlic. Next add lemon juice, broth and Burgundy wine to the cooking bag. Add your seasoned roast and close the oven bag with nylon tie. Cut 6¹/₂ inch slits in the bag and bake for 2¹/₂ hours or until tender. Remove your venison roast to one or two large serving platters. Strain bag/pan drippings into a bowl and pass with the pieces of savory venison roast.

OUR FAVORITE CROCK POT VENISON STROGANOFF

2 to 2¹/₂ pounds venison roast
3 tablespoons butter
4 oz. mushrooms, sliced
1 small onion, chopped
¹/₂ cup catsup
1 tablespoon Worcestershire sauce
2 teaspoons salt

1 teaspoon celery seed
1 teaspoon black pepper
1 cup beef bouillon
3 to 4 drops Tabasco or hot sauce
2 tablespoons butter
2 tablespoons flour
1 cup sour cream

Heat 3 tablespoons butter in skillet and brown venison on all sides. Combine other ingredients, except last three, in slow cooker and add browned venison roast. Cook on low heat for 8 hours. Then in sauce pan melt 2 tablespoons butter and add flour and ¹/₂ cup juices from cooker. Blend; then add sour cream. Return to cooker and stir well. Simmer 15 minutes and serve venison over bow ties or noodles. Delicious!

We know from experience venison jerky is a big favorite of Pennsylvanians. Try making this summer sausage and see if this is not a favorite you will want to make every year.

HOMEMADE VENISON SUMMER SAUSAGE

3 pounds ground venison
2 tablespoons tender quick salt, or tenderizer
2 teaspoons garlic salt
1 teaspoon ground red pepper
2 pounds ground pork

2¹/₂ teaspoons mustard
2 teaspoons black pepper
2 teaspoons hickory-smoke salt
1 teaspoon chili powder

Mix all ingredients and cover. Place in refrigerator for 24 hours. Mix again. Cover and place in refrigerator for 24 more hours. Make 5 rolls. Bake in oven on broiler pan for 6-8 hours at 200 degrees. Sample at 6 hours and take it out when you feel it is done. Let stand covered in refrigerator a day or two, then double wrap each loaf separately and freeze.

*W*e Aim To Please! If you are looking for that always "special recipe" venison stew, look <u>no further</u>. You've got to prepare this <u>easy</u> recipe. Serve with hot buttered bread or garlic bread and your favorite red wine for a <u>memorable</u> meal.

GALE'S CROCKPOT VENISON STEW

2¹/₂ pounds venison stew meat, cubed

2 carrots, sliced

3 stalks celery, sliced

1 cup tomatoes, crushed or stewed

1 cup onions, chopped

3 garlic cloves, diced

1 teaspoon red pepper flakes, optional

1 bay leaf

1 teaspoon each salt and black pepper

1 teaspoon Italian seasoning

1 teaspoon parsley

1 cup red wine - not cooking wine

1 (10 oz.) can golden or cream of mushroom soup

1 (14 oz.) can beef broth

1 (12 oz.) jar roasted peppers, drained and chopped

1 (15 oz.) can Italian Cannellini beans or Garbonzo beans

Spray 4-5 quart slow cooker bowl with non-stick spray. Add cubed and trimmed venison. Add carrots, celery, tomatoes, onions, garlic and red pepper flakes if using. Add remaining seasonings and stir in wine, soup and beef broth, stir well. Cover and slow cook on high for 6 hours. After 6 hours add chopped roasted peppers and can of Cannellini or Garbonzo beans. Add water if needed. Stir well and slow cook 1-2 more hours or until the venison is cooked - Tender!

GALE'S VENISON STUFFED MUSHROOMS APPETIZER

30 medium mushrooms (1½ pounds)

vegetable cooking spray

½ pound venisonburger or sausage

¼ cup chopped green onions

1 clove garlic, minced

¼ cup soft bread crumbs

1 egg, beaten

2 tablespoons grated Parmesan cheese

½ teaspoon dried Italian seasoning

Clean mushrooms, remove stems and chop finely; set aside mushroom caps. Spray a large skillet with vegetable spray. Add venison, onions, garlic and mushroom stems, cooking until venison is brown. Stir in bread crumbs, egg, cheese and Italian seasoning. Spoon burger or sausage mixture into mushroom caps. Bake at 350 degrees for 10 minutes. When the venison stuffed mushrooms are done, put on serving plate with tooth picks and serve hot. Tasty!

SLOW-COOKER VENISON GUMBO

¼ to ½ cup flour

1 teaspoon each salt and black pepper

1¼ to 1½ pounds venison in 1 inch cubes

3 to 4 garlic cloves, diced

3 to 4 tablespoons butter

½ pound smoke sausage, sliced

2 (6½ oz.) cans minced clams

2 (4½ oz.) cans tiny shrimp

2 bay leaves

4 tablespoons clam juice

1 (10 oz.) pkg. frozen okra or broccoli

2 cups onions, chopped

1 green pepper, chopped

½ cup white wine

cayenne pepper to taste

enough water to cover by 2-3 inches

Put flour seasoned with salt and black pepper and venison in plastic bag and shake to coat. In a large frying pan brown venison chunks with diced garlic in butter (10 to 15 minutes). Add venison, sliced smoked sausage, clams and shrimp to your slow cooker. Stir and add bay leaves, clam juice, okra, onions, green pepper, wine, cayenne pepper to taste, and stir. Add enough water to cover. Cook on low heat 8 to 10 hours or on high heat 6 to 7 hours. Serve over rice or enjoy as is. Pass the French bread, please!

Venison Stew With Navy Beans

1/2 pound dried navy beans

1 pound venison round steak, cubed or stew meat, cubed

2 cloves garlic, diced

2 tablespoons olive oil

1 large green pepper, chopped

1 large onion, chopped

1 teaspoon Italian seasoning

1 teaspoon chili powder

3 fresh mushrooms, sliced

1 can tomato soup

1 teaspoon salt

1 teaspoon black pepper

In a medium pan soak navy beans overnight in enough water to cover by 2 inches; adding more water later if needed. Next morning drain and fill pan with enough water to cover your beans. Bring beans to a boil then reduce heat and simmer them for 2 hours or so until soft. In a large Dutch oven brown venison cubes and garlic in two tablespoons olive oil for 10 to 15 minutes. Chop and add the green pepper, onions, Italian seasoning, and chili powder; stir and simmer 10 minutes. Add sliced mushrooms, tomato soup, salt, black pepper, and beans with water from the other pan to your venison in Dutch oven. Turn up the heat to medium and then simmer 30 minutes or until hot enough to serve. Serve in bowls as is with your favorite bread or serve over rice or noodles. Add cayenne pepper or Tabasco sauce if you prefer to spice this meal up even more to your taste. As always, enjoy!

WINTER HOLIDAY BARBECUE VENISON

Place in a large oven roaster:

**4 to 5 pounds venison hind
  quarter roast**
1/4 cup liquid smoke
1 1/2 teaspoon garlic powder
1/2 teaspoon cayenne pepper

1/4 cup minced onion
1 teaspoon salt
1/2 teaspoon black pepper
1 1/2 cups water

Cover and bake in a 275 degree oven until fork tender, about 5 to 6 hours. Remove venison and reserve 1 cup juices. Chill for easier slicing later.

In same roaster on top of range, blend and simmer the following for 10 to 15 minutes:

1 bottle (20 oz.) catsup
1 jar (20 oz.) salsa
1 cup reserved juices
**3/4 cup firmly packed brown
  sugar**
1/4 cup Worcestershire sauce
2 tablespoons white vinegar

**2 teaspoons prepared
  mustard**
1 1/2 teaspoons celery salt
1 teaspoon minced onion
1 teaspoon salt
1/2 teaspoon garlic powder
1/2 teaspoon black pepper

Add thinly sliced venison back to the above sauce. Heat through 15 to 20 minutes. Delicious! Pass the barbecue beans and tossed salad, please. Let it snow, enjoy!

T his is a mild flavored chili, so if you prefer, add some canned Jalepeno peppers or additional red pepper flakes to taste to spice it up. Tip—spicier is not always better!

STEVE'S VENISON CHILI

1 pound venisonburger or sausage

1 large onion, chopped (about 2 cups)

2 (15½ oz.) cans dark red kidney beans, undrained - or chili beans

1 (4 oz.) can mushrooms

3 (14½ oz.) cans chili-style chunky tomatoes, undrained

1 teaspoon garlic powder

1 teaspoon parsley

1 teaspoon dried oregano, crushed

½ teaspoon ground red pepper

½ teaspoon black pepper

1 tablespoon chili powder

Cook the ground venisonburger or sausage and chopped onion in a Dutch oven until the venison is brown and the onion is tender. Stir in the undrained beans, mushrooms, and the undrained tomatoes. Add the garlic powder, parsley, oregano, ground red pepper, black pepper, and chili powder. Bring the mixture to boiling; reduce heat. Simmer, uncovered, about 1½ hours or until chili reaches desired consistency, stirring occasionally. Pass the biscuits please, MMM Good!

*A*fter preparing this uniquely spice venison jerky we
really liked it, but we sough out unbiased opinions
from our friends, Harry and Rich at the barber shop.
Then we asked our friends, Brian, Rob, Don and
Renae at Print King to sample it. All raved about it,
so we know you will, too.

STEVE'S FAVORITE VENISON JERKY

1 or 1½ cups soy sauce

½ cup Worcestershire sauce

1 tablespoon "hot sauce"

½ cup burgundy wine

¼ cup lemon juice

½ cup red wine

1 tablespoon liquid smoke

1 teaspoon onion powder

4 garlic cloves (large), diced

1 cup brown sugar

½ teaspoon allspice

1 teaspoon black pepper

3 pounds venison stew meat,
thinly sliced into small 2-3
inch strips

Mix the above ingredients, except venison, in a large glass bowl or
baking dish and stir to blend. Add sliced venison strips and stir to
coat completely. Cover and marinate for 18-24 hours, turning a time
or two to marinate all venison completely. To prepare, follow your
dehydrator instructions and enjoy. Since we do not have a dehydrator we use two large non-stick baking pans and our oven. Bake venison jerky at 180-200 degrees from 4-5 hours, turning once. Remove
from oven when the jerky is sampled and dried out as you like it.
Venison jerky will dry out more the first 2-3 days in your refrigerator.

Tip: If you like it "hot" sprinkle with cayenne pepper on individual
portions to taste.

*T*his festive-looking dish is perfect for a dish to pass at holiday time. I fixed this dish for my husband and me the day before Christmas as a special treat. It served the two of us as a one-dish meal with enough left over to enjoy another day. Very Good Indeed . . . . .

GALE'S HOLIDAY VENISON ITALIAN PIE

1 unbaked 9-inch pastry shell

3/4 pound venisonburger or sausage

3/4 cup chopped green bell pepper

3/4 cup mushrooms, sliced

1 medium clove garlic, minced

1 cup water

6 oz. tomato paste

1 1/2 teaspoon Italian seasoning

1/2 teaspoon oregano

1/2 teaspoon sage

1/2 teaspoon chili powder

1 teaspoon salt

1 (10 oz.) pkg. frozen broccoli, thawed and well drained

2/3 cup ricotta cheese

1 cup shredded mozzarella cheese

1 cup chopped fresh tomato

Line pastry shell with a double thickness of foil. Bake in a 450 degree oven for 5 to 8 minutes (depending on thickness of pastry). Remove foil. Bake 3 to 4 minutes more or until set and dry; set aside.

In a medium skillet cook venisonburger or sausage, green pepper, mushrooms, and garlic until venison is brown and vegetables are tender. Stir in water, tomato paste, Italian seasoning, oregano, sage, chili powder, and salt. Heat to boiling; reduce heat and simmer, covered, for 10 minutes. Meanwhile, in a medium bowl stir together broccoli, ricotta cheese, and 1/4 cup of the mozzarella cheese. Spoon the broccoli filling into baked pastry shell. Top with venison mixture. Cover edge of pastry with foil to prevent over-browning. Bake in a 350 degree oven for 30 minutes. Remove foil. Top with tomato and remaining 3/4 cup mozzarella cheese. Bake 15 minutes more or until heated through and tomato is cooked. Let stand 10 minutes before serving.

*A*ccording to dates in my hunters' cookbook we have been enjoying this recipe annually since 1990. Try it ... you will like it. You can use any venison sausage recipe you like. Try this special dish over the holidays when it can be made ahead and reheated when needed. Enjoy! Troy Burkett, a friend of ours, called us after trying this quiche saying it was just awesome . . . . . .

OUR FAVORITE VENISON SAUSAGE QUICHE

2 (9-inch) size pie shells

1 pound venison sausage, use our recipe on facing page or any venison sausage

A little olive oil

1 pound fresh mushrooms, sliced

¹/₃ cup onions, chopped

3 large eggs

8 oz. Monterey Jack cheese, grated

8 oz. heavy whipping cream

¹/₂ teaspoon each salt and pepper

Bake two ready to bake pie shells according to directions. Preheat the oven to 350 degrees so it is ready for quiche. Brown venison sausage for 10 minutes or so; remove to a large bowl to drain any fat. To the same frying pan add olive oil if needed and fry mushrooms and onions. Remove the fat from the large bowl and to venison sausage add mushrooms, onions, eggs, cheese, heavy whipping cream, salt and pepper. With a large spoon mix thoroughly and spoon into two baked pie crusts. Bake at 350 degrees for 30 minutes.

OLD-TIME VENISON SAUSAGE

5 pounds ground venison
5 pounds ground pork butt
1 to 2 tablespoons sage
2 teaspoons thyme
1 3/4 teaspoon crushed red
  pepper
2 tablespoons fennel seeds

3 cloves garlic, minced
2 to 4 tablespoons salt
1 to 2 tablespoons freshly
  ground pepper
2 tablespoons onion flakes
2 tablespoons Italian
  seasoning

Grind you own venison from trimmed deer front shoulder. Do it yourself or have a butcher grind it for you and give it back fresh. Stop at a grocer and have them grind a 5+ pound pork butt roast up for you. You now have to mix 1/2 the venison with 1/2 ground pork and 1/2 seasonings. Then mix meat and seasonings of other half. Now mix each 5 pound pan thoroughly together to have total of 10 pounds venison sausage. Roll into 10 one pound balls or loaves onto freezer paper. Wrap each with plastic freezer wrap and drop into one quart freezer bags for quality freezer protection. Lean and tasty!

 A DEER HUNTER'S WIFE KNOWS!
When my husband carefully field dresses his deer, quick cools the venison by skinning the deer and then processes the venison by hand as soon as possible the venison is NEVER GAMY. In fact, it is one of the most delicious and healthy red meats you can serve to your family.

*W*e think you must try this recipe soon. We first prepared this recipe while living in Memphis, TN years ago. Barbecue beef and pork are very popular there. This recipe is delicious and was selected for inclusion in the NRA's wild game cookbook in 1992. It was also the Grand Prize winning recipe in the Cranberry Journal's Holiday Cook-off in 1996.

STEVE'S VENISON BARBECUE

BARBECUE SAUCE:

2 sticks butter

8 oz. tomato sauce

1 teaspoon black pepper

1/2 cup lemon juice

1/2 teaspoon oregano

1/2 teaspoon dry mustard

1/2 teaspoon thyme

1/2 teaspoon Worcestershire sauce

dash of liquid smoke

1/2 cup chopped onion

1/2 cup catsup

1/2 teaspoon garlic salt

1/2 teaspoon rosemary

1/2 teaspoon salt

Heat two sticks butter in a one quart saucepan. Add remaining ingredients and simmer 10 minutes.

1 pound sweet or hot Italian bulk sausage

1 1/2 to 2 pounds venison roast or steak

1/2 cup all-purpose flour (minimum)

1 teaspoon seasoned salt

1 teaspoon black pepper

1 (4 oz.) can mushrooms

2 stalks fresh celery, chopped

1/2 large onion sliced

1/2 cup red wine

1 green pepper, sliced

barbecue sauce (see above)

1/2 teaspoon red pepper (optional)

Fry bulk sausage in Dutch oven and remove to a bowl, leaving drippings in pan and set aside. Cube roast or steak, dredge in flour seasoned with seasoned salt and black pepper. Fry pieces of cubed venison in Dutch oven until brown. Simmer for 30 minutes. Return sausage to pan of venison and add mushrooms, celery, onion, wine, green pepper, barbecue sauce, red pepper (optional) and any left over flour. Stir well and simmer 40 to 50 minutes or until tender. Serve over your favorite rice with hot bread.

LODER'S SPECIALTY OF "THE HOUSE"

1 (2 to 2¹/₂) pound hind quarter roast

2 tablespoons soy sauce

2 tablespoons Worcestershire sauce

¹/₄ cup red wine - *not cooking wine!*

2 to 3 garlic cloves, diced

1 teaspoon prepared mustard

¹/₂ teaspoon salt

¹/₄ teaspoon each black and cayenne pepper

1 teaspoon onion powder

Place your venison roast in a baking dish and poke numerous holes with a knife on both sides. Add remaining ingredients, toss several times, and cover with plastic wrap. Let stand over night in refrigerator and in the morning turn venison over to marinade until time to bake or grill that afternoon or evening. Bake this savory venison dish at 350 degrees for 45 minutes or so to medium rare at its best. *Tender and juicy* ....

Grilling option: Grill to medium rare using a spatula for turning so you sear in your venison juices. Baste often with marinade. Save left over venison roast and add it to your favorite tossed salad and dressing for another tasty venison meal.

*I*f you like olives and roasted peppers, this venison sauce is uniquely delicious. May substitute olives with 10 oz. frozen vegetable of your choice. So - so good!

PASTA SPECIALTY OF OUR HOUSE

1 pound venisonburger or sausage

1 (12 oz.) jar roasted peppers

2 (8 oz.) cans tomato sauce

1 large (6 oz.) can large black olives, cut in half

3 cloves garlic, diced

2-3 tablespoons Romano or Parmesan cheese

1 cup barbecue sauce or salsa

1 cup green onions, chopped

4 cups fresh or canned tomatoes, chopped

2 to 3 cups water, for preferred thickness

1 teaspoon each salt, black pepper, oregano and parsley

In a large frying pan add venisonburger or sausage and drain olive oil from roasted peppers, adding to venison. Brown venison 15 to 20 minutes. Then drain and add to slow cooker. Add remaining ingredients, stir and cook on high for 6 to 7 hours or low 8 to 10 hours. Serve over as much as a pound of your favorite pasta.

EASILY OUR BEST VENISON SOUP

1 pound venison steak, cubed small or a pound of venisonburger or sausage
1 cup onions, diced
2 cloves garlic, diced
2 tablespoons butter
1 (10 oz.) pkg. frozen broccoli, chopped
1 (10 oz.) pkg. frozen okra
2 cups celery, diced

3 1/2 oz. jar (hot) Jalapeno peppers or (mild) green chili peppers
1 can your favorite cream of soup
1 cup fresh mushrooms, sliced
1 (46 oz.) can tomato juice or 6 cups stewed tomatoes
1 teaspoon salt
1/2 teaspoon black pepper

In a skillet brown venison with onions and garlic in 2 tablespoons butter. Spray a 4-5 quart slow cooker with non-stick spray and add browned venison. Then add broccoli, okra, celery and Jalapeno or chili peppers, then stir to blend. Add cream of soup, mushrooms, tomato juice, or stewed tomatoes, salt and pepper, and stir. Cook on low for 7-8 hours or on high 5-6 hours. Serve with hot buttered bread as is or add baked sweet potatoes for an even more nutritious meal.

VENISON SALISBURY STEAKBURGERS

A hearty flavor to satisfy hungry hunters.

1 1/2 pounds ground venisonburger
6 tablespoons steak sauce
1/2 teaspoon salt
1/4 teaspoon black pepper

1 can (10 1/2 oz.) condensed onion or golden mushroom soup
1/2 cup catsup or Picante sauce

In medium bowl, combine venison, 4 tablespoons steak sauce, salt and pepper. Shape into 4 burgers. In large skillet, brown burgers on both sides. In small bowl, combine remaining steak sauce, soup, and catsup or Picante sauce. Pour over burgers. Simmer, covered 10 minutes or until steakburgers are cooked as desired. Serve, garnished with sautéed mushrooms and your favorite vegetable. We suggest baked sweet potatoes.

S teve had this recipe the first time when hunting deer at Hankin's deer camp in Mississippi. The camp chef gave him his recipe. We really like it and you will, too.

UP THE HOLLOW VENISON ROUND STEAK

1 medium onion, sliced
1/2 cup chopped celery
5 tablespoons butter
1 1/2 pounds venison steak, cut in 1 inch thick cubes
3 tablespoons flour
1 teaspoon salt
1/2 teaspoon black pepper

1/2 teaspoon chili powder
1 pound can whole tomatoes
2 teaspoons prepared mustard
1 teaspoon sugar
1 teaspoon leaf marjoram
1/2 green pepper, sliced
2 cloves garlic, diced

In large skillet sauté onion and celery in melted butter about 5 minutes; remove from butter and set aside. Cut venison steak into serving pieces. Combine flour, salt, black pepper, and chili powder. Dip meat into seasoned flour. Brown venison steak in butter in skillet. Combine tomatoes, mustard, sugar, and marjoram. Pour over venison. Top with green pepper, garlic, and add onion, and celery. Cover and simmer 60 minutes or until tender. Great tasting steak!

OUR VENISON BREAKFAST CASSEROLE

1 pound bulk venison
sausage

1 cup seasoned croutons
(cheddar or herb)

2 cups (8 oz.) shredded
cheddar cheese, divided

1 teaspoon garlic salt or garlic
powder

1 teaspoon chili powder

1 teaspoon onion flakes

1 teaspoon Italian seasoning

1 teaspoon spicy mustard

8 eggs

Preheat oven to 325 degrees. Over medium heat brown venison sausage and set aside in a bowl. Grease a 7 x 11 inch glass baking dish so as not to stick. Cover the bottom with coarsely crumbled croutons and sprinkle in 1 cup cheddar cheese. To your bowl of venison add above seasonings; stir. Now crack and add eggs and mix well. With a large spoon spread seasoned venison sausage over crouton/cheese mix in baking dish. Lastly top casserole with remaining cup of cheddar cheese. Bake 20-25 minutes so eggs are lightly browned and set. If desired serve with toasted Italian bread and salsa on the side. As always, enjoy this *large* family breakfast.

*S*pecial thanks to none other than Sheryn Jones, our cookbook consultant, for her recipe. It's an easy and delicious dish!

SHERYN'S MARINATED VENISON ROAST

1 1/2 to 2 pounds venison
roast, cooked

2 onions, sliced into rings

2 (4 1/2 oz.) jars mushrooms,
drained

1 (3 1/2 oz.) jar capers

sugar to taste

salt to taste

pepper to taste

1/4 cup red wine vinegar

3/4 cup salad oil

Cut cooked venison into bite-size pieces. Layer venison, onion rings, mushrooms and capers. Season with sugar, salt and pepper. Mix with vinegar and oil. (Increase proportions if needed to cover layered pieces). Refrigerate at least a day or two before serving. Serve cold with tossed, potato, or macaroni salad .... *Very good, indeed!*

*F*inally, on a day off from work, Mark and I would hunt
a day together. We would climb the mountain near
his home before daylight and I would hunt for a fall turkey
while he would bow hunt for deer. It was an uneventful
morning for me but by 2 P.M., as luck would have it I was
helping Mark locate a buck he hit. After I found his 6
point I agreed to do Mark and his family a favor by hand
processing his buck for them. I used some of his venison to
prepare this meal for them when I delivered his venison for
wrapping and freezing. This meal brought smiles and
complements all around .... ENJOY!
P.S. Be sure to read the deer tale about this hunt titled,
The Six Point that Did Not Get Away.

MARK'S BUCK IN A BAG

1 large size Reynolds oven
  cooking bag
2 tablespoons flour
1/3 cup Italian salad dressing
1 pkg. Lipton's savory herb
  and garlic soup
1 teaspoon each salt and
  black pepper
1 small onion, chopped

2 carrots, chopped
2 celery stalks, chopped
1 pound of potatoes, cubed or
  sliced
5-6 fresh mushroom caps,
  sliced
3/4 cup liquid; water, salsa, or
  catsup
2 pounds of venison steak or
  roast, cubed

Preheat oven to 350 degrees. Place your large cooking bag in a 9 x
13 inch baking dish; add flour, seal and shake bag to coat. Add
dressing, dry soup packet, salt and pepper. Seal and shake bag to
blend spices. Then add chopped onions, carrots, celery, potatoes,
and mushrooms. Seal bag and shake to mix spices and vegetables.
Lastly add 3/4 cup liquid of your choice and cubed venison. Seal bag
and shake to coat venison. Then seal bag with a twist tie and use a
knife to cut 6-7 holes in the top of the roasting bag. Bake 90 minutes; then remove dish to cool 15-20 minutes on the stove before
opening to serve. One taste of this venison will bring smiles all
around home or camp!

GALE'S VENISON & VEGETABLE STEW

1 pound boneless venison
   steak, cut in 3/4 inch cubes

2 tablespoons olive oil

2½ cups beef broth

2 med. zucchini, halved
   lengthwise, sliced

2 stalks celery, chopped

1 large onion, cut into wedges

2 medium carrots, thinly
   sliced

½ green pepper, chopped
   (½ cup)

1 bay leaf

½ teaspoon sugar

1 teaspoon chili powder

2 cloves garlic, diced

1 teaspoon dried Italian
   seasoning

½ teaspoon black pepper

1 (6 oz.) can tomato paste

In a large frying pan brown cubed venison in 2 tablespoons of olive oil. To your crock pot add venison, beef broth, vegetables, spices and tomato paste. Stir well and cook on a low setting for 6 to 8 hours or on a high setting for 4 to 5 hours. Thicken your stew with half cup water and 2 tablespoons of flour if desired; cook another 30 minutes before serving. Mix well and enjoy a nutritious venison and vegetable meal.

 A DEER HUNTER'S WIFE KNOWS!

It has been years since our family has had to go without venison, but the one year we did, is easy to recall because we missed not having those tasty venison dishes that we had come to enjoy year in and year out. That is what made us prepare the Loder Family Favorite recipe selections for you in both our cookbooks, Quality Venison *and* Quality Venison II. *We know you will want to prepare these favorites first. They can't miss.*

Gale and I had this venison dish to celebrate on the day our first Quality Venison cookbook was printed and was shipped to us. It was a deliciously fitting celebration meal. Try it and you will see.

DAD'S CELEBRATION VENISON

1½ pounds venison round or loin steak, thinly sliced

salt to taste

1 teaspoon garlic powder

½ teaspoon black pepper

2 tablespoons cider vinegar

2 tablespoons olive oil or butter

1 onion, sliced in rings or strips

1 green pepper sliced in rings or strips

1 small jar or can mushrooms

1 (14½ oz.) can beef broth, divided *

½ cup red wine (your choice) Rosé or Burgundy

2 tablespoons cornstarch

Your favorite pasta prepared for 6

Season your sliced venison steak in a dish with salt, garlic powder, black pepper and vinegar. Coat a large heated skillet or wok with 2 tablespoons of olive oil or butter, and brown venison. Add onion and green pepper strips; sauté. Then add mushrooms, beef broth *(reserving ¼ cup) and red wine. Mix cornstarch with ¼ cup reserved beef broth; add to skillet or wok and stir until thickened. Serve this savory venison dish over your favorite pasta. Enjoy! Thanks, Dad, for your recipe from years gone by.

Dad's Cheesy Venison Casserole

A tasty venison dish for family or deer camp.
Do not anticipate leftovers ......

4 cups *cooked* small pasta (2 cups dry)

1 pound venisonburger or sausage

2/3 cup green onions, chopped

2 garlic cloves, diced

3 tablespoons olive oil

1 (4 oz.) can tomato soup

1 cup water

1/2 cup catsup

1/2 teaspoon black pepper

1 1/2 cups shredded cheddar cheese (divided in half)

Preheat your oven to 350 degrees, and cook pasta to package directions. In a large skillet brown venison over medium heat with onions and garlic in 3 tablespoons olive oil, stirring to separate until done. Stir in pasta, soup, water, catsup, pepper, half of the shredded cheddar cheese. Stir and then pour mixture into a one and a half quart casserole dish. Top with remaining cheese. Bake uncovered 35 to 40 minutes until hot and bubbling.

Try this easy, tasty dish if you need a special meal for two. So ... Good ... There will not be any leftovers!

Gale's Easy Venison Parmesan

8 oz. your favorite pasta

1 cup stewed tomatoes

1 pound venison loin steaks

1 garlic clove, minced

1 teaspoon Italian seasoning

1/2 teaspoon salt

1 teaspoon minced onion flakes

1/2 teaspoon black pepper

1/2 cup tomato sauce

1 cup shredded Parmesan cheese

Cook pasta according to package directions and set aside. Spray an appropriate size baking dish (6 x 10) with non-stick cooking spray. Add stewed tomatoes and top with venison steaks. Then add remaining seasonings; top with tomato sauce. Sprinkle 1 cup of Parmesan cheese across the top. Now bake venison at 350 degrees for 40-45 minutes. Serve over pasta. Now that's Italian ....

If you are looking for a light, but delicious meal-in-one-dish, this is the one for you. When baking, it fills your house with a wonderful aroma, and it tastes as good, if not better than it smells. We would not hesitate to serve this meal to even finicky eaters. Try it and you will be glad you did.

GALE'S DELIGHTFULLY LIGHT VENISON NOODLE BAKE

1 pound venisonburger or sausage

1 (8 oz.) can tomato sauce, or salsa

4 cups (8 oz.) noodles, cooked and drained

1/2 pound Velveeta Light Pasteurized Cheese Spread, cubed

1 cup light cottage cheese

1/3 cup green onion sices

2 tablespoons chopped green pepper

1/2 cup Parmesan or Romano cheese

onion and garlic powder to taste (optional)

Brown venisonburger or sausage. Add tomato sauce or salsa. Layer half of the noodles and process cheese spread In 10 x 6 inch baking dish. Top with combined cottage cheese, onion and green pepper. Repeat noodle and process cheese spread layers. Top with meat mixture and 1/2 cup Parmesan or Romano cheese, slong with onion and garlic powder if using. Bake at 350 degrees for 30 minutes.

PREPARING
VENISON
MARINADES & SAUCES

*O*ur *family loves venison on the grill or smoker with just salt and pepper seasoning. But I really enjoyed creating, using and testing most of the recipes in this section on our venison over the years.*

Be creative and feel free to substitute, change or add seasonings to your tastes. We generally prepare sauces and marinades the day before grilling. When our schedule allows us to plan ahead of time we will marinate venison or put it in the sauce we've made up overnight or until smoking or grilling time. Otherwise we follow recipe directions for time.

SOME OF OUR FAVORITE VENISON MARINADES

We have used these marinade recipes to flavor 2 pounds of venison steak or 3 to 4 pound hind quarter roast.

Marinades are fun — enjoy new tastes! Let's make it simple or standard for each recipe: Combine listed ingredients. Place venison in any zipper lock plastic bag and pour in your marinade. Remove air from bag and seal. Refrigerate 1 hour or overnight, your choice. Extending marinating time does further tenderize the venison. Brush on venison steaks, roasts, or burgers while grilling.

DAD'S ITALIAN MELODY

1/2 cup olive oil

1/2 cup lemon juice

3 cloves garlic, diced

1/2 teaspoon each salt and pepper

1 teaspoon Italian seasoning

SAVORY VENISON MARINADE

14 oz. can beef broth

2 tablespoons red wine

2 tablespoons Worcestershire sauce

1 tablespoon olive oil

1 tablespoon Italian seasoning

STEVE'S SUNNY VENISON MARINADE

1 (12 oz.) can frozen orange juice concentrate, thawed

3/4 cup soy sauce

1/3 cup honey

2 1/2 teaspoons ground ginger

PITTSBURGH PIZZAZZ

1/2 cup Chablis wine

1/2 cup Dijon or spicy mustard

2 tablespoons olive oil

2 tablespoons lemon juice

1 teaspoon oregano or basil

RAYLAND'S VENISON STEAK BASTING SAUCE

1/3 cup red wine or cider
   vinegar
1/3 cup olive oil
1 teaspoon soy sauce
1/2 teaspoon cayenne pepper

1/3 cup lemon juice
1 teaspoon onion flakes
1 teaspoon black pepper
1 teaspoon salt

Combine ingredients in small sauce pan and simmer 10 to 15 minutes. Brush venison with sauce while grilling. Be careful not to over cook.

DAD'S VENISON GRAVY

3 tablespoons olive oil
1/3 cup chopped carrot
1/3 cup chopped onion
2 cloves garlic, diced
4 tablespoons minced parsley

1 cup dry red wine
2 1/2 cups canned beef gravy
1 1/2 teaspoons ground black
   pepper

Pour oil in skillet and heat. Then sauté carrots, onion, garlic, and parsley about 5 minutes. Add wine and simmer 5 minutes. Add gravy and black pepper and cook over low heat about half an hour, until carrots are soft. This is a traditional gravy to serve with broiled or fried venison steaks.

MARINADE SAUCE FOR BARBECUE VENISON KABOBS

3 to 4 pounds venison round
   steak cut into 3/4 to 1 inch
   squares
3 cups catsup or chili sauce
   or salsa

1 cup honey
1 cup soy sauce
1 cup sugar
1 cup vinegar

In a bowl mix all ingredients well, except venison. Add venison to sauce. Marinate venison in sauce in refrigerator for 8 hours or overnight. Stir venison before pinching them onto the skewers for grilling. Baste venison kabobs while grilling. Cook to medium rare so kabobs are juicy. ENJOY!

COUNTRY STYLE BARBECUE SAUCE

3/4 cup water

2 medium onions, sliced

2 tablespoons brown sugar

1/2 teaspoon dried mustard

1/2 teaspoon black pepper

2 tablespoons Worcestershire sauce

8 oz. tomato sauce

1 teaspoon garlic powder or 2 cloves garlic, diced

1/4 cup each lemon juice, vinegar, and catsup

1 teaspoon salt

Mix all and simmer 10 minutes. Delicious over any venison, beef or pork also.

APPALACHIAN MOUNTAIN SAUCE

1/2 cup brown sugar

1/2 cup cider or red wine vinegar

2 tablespoons prepared mustard

1 tablespoon olive or vegetable oil

2 cloves garlic, minced

3/4 cup catsup

1/3 cup chili sauce or salsa

2 tablespoons steak sauce

dash hot pepper or Tabasco sauce

In a small bowl, combine all ingredients; mix well. Baste steaks or venisonburgers. Makes enough for grilling or smoking 2 pounds of venison.

QUICK BARBECUE SAUCE

1 cup orange marmalade

1 1/2 cups your choice - salsa

1 teaspoon onion salt

1/4 cup red wine vinegar

1 tablespoon Worcestershire sauce

1 tablespoon soy sauce

Mix marmalade, salsa, onion salt, vinegar, Worcestershire, and soy sauce. Use to baste venison steaks, roasts, or venisonburgers. Makes about 2 cups.

ROSÉ WINE MARINADE

1/2 cup Rosé wine, (slightly sweet)
1/2 cup vegetable oil
2 cloves garlic, minced
1/2 teaspoon ground ginger or thyme

1/2 cup soy sauce
2 tablespoons lemon juice
1 teaspoon salt
1/2 teaspoon black pepper

In a bowl, combine all ingredients; blend well. Place steak in a double plastic bag. Pour marinade over venison. Seal and refrigerate several hours or overnight, turning venison occasionally. Grill steak to desired doneness. Best venison steak medium rare to medium. Trust me!

RED WINE MARINADE

Venison is a lean, rich meat so do not cook too well done or it will be tough and dry. Steak best medium rare or pink in middle. Keep in mind that an older deer will have tougher venison steaks, so double the time it marinates turning several times.

1 cup red wine
1/4 cup minced celery
2 cloves garlic, minced
1 teaspoon crushed thyme leaf

1/2 cup olive oil
1/4 cup minced onion
1 teaspoon crushed parsley or Italian seasoning
1/2 teaspoon black pepper

In a bowl, combine all ingredients; blend well. Place venison in a shallow dish. Poke through venison 8-10 times with knife. Pour marinade over venison. Cover and refrigerate 3 to 4 hours. Grill as desired.

*W*e first came across a great venison marinade recipe
similar to this over ten years ago. It was modified
some to season it a little more to our taste and cooking
preference. We think it is great so give it a try
on your venison soon!

THE BEST STEAK MARINADE

1 1/2 cups salad oil

1/4 cup Worcestershire sauce

2 teaspoon salt

1 teaspoon black pepper

1/2 cup wine vinegar

1/3 cup lemon juice

3/4 cup soy sauce

2 teaspoon dry mustard

1 1/2 teaspoon parsley flakes

1/2 cup red wine

1-2 cloves garlic, minced

1/2 teaspoon cayenne pepper
(optional)

Makes 3 1/2 cups. Keep in refrigerator in tightly covered jar and use
as needed. Marinade meat 2-4 hours in frig. Turn several times.
Grill or fry venison steak. Wow! Enjoy!

NEW ORLEANS BARBECUE SAUCE

1 teaspoon black or cayenne
pepper

2 ounces bourbon or red wine
vinegar

2 tablespoons Worcestershire
sauce

1 cup water

2 teaspoons soy sauce

1 teaspoon garlic powder

In a small bowl, combine all ingredients. Brush on venison steaks
or venisonburgers during grilling.

*W*e made this barbecue sauce in the morning of our
daughter, Kelly's 21st birthday. We poured it over
venison tender loin and marinated it for 4 hours, turning
several times. We basted the loin steak while grilling.
Reheat remaining sauce and serve with grilled loin steak.
You'll love this sauce, so mark the recipe page.
You will be back again and again.

SMOKY BARBECUE SAUCE

1 teaspoon salt

1 can (10³/₄ oz.) tomato soup, undiluted

¹/₄ cup catsup or chili sauce

2 tablespoons liquid smoke

1 tablespoon Worcestershire sauce

¹/₂ teaspoon garlic powder

1 cup packed brown sugar

¹/₄ cup butter

2 tablespoons prepared mustard

2 tablespoons lemon juice

1 teaspoon onion powder

1 teaspoon black pepper

In a medium saucepan, combine all ingredients; blend well. Bring
to boiling over low heat, stirring frequently. Boil 1 minute; remove
from heat. Brush on venisonburgers or steaks to taste.
*Makes enough for 1¹/₂ to 2 pounds venison.

ROG'S BURGUNDY MARINADE

1 cup Burgundy wine
1/2 cup olive oil
2 large cloves garlic, diced
1 teaspoon dried thyme

1 teaspoon onion powder
1 teaspoon black pepper
1/2 teaspoon dried parsley
salt to taste

In a bowl mix wine, oil, garlic, thyme, onion powder, pepper, parsley, and salt. Use to marinate venison before cooking, and to baste during cooking. Makes 1 1/2 cups.

RICK'S VENISON BARBECUE SAUCE

1/3 cup olive oil
1/4 cup onion, minced
1/2 teaspoon hot red or black pepper
1/2 cup Burgundy or Rosé wine

2 garlic cloves, diced
1/2 teaspoon salt
1/2 teaspoon Italian seasoning
1/2 cup chili sauce or salsa

Combine all ingredients and cook on medium heat to near boiling. Reduce heat and simmer 10-15 minutes. Great basting sauce on venisonburgers or steak!

A TENNESSEE BARBECUE SAUCE

3 cans (8 oz. each) tomato sauce
3 cups water
1 cup white vinegar
1 bottle Worcestershire sauce
1 teaspoon seasoned salt

1 teaspoon dry mustard
2 teaspoons soy sauce
3/4 cup brown sugar
cayenne pepper to taste
1 teaspoon chili powder
1 teaspoon garlic powder

Blend together tomato sauce, water, vinegar, Worcestershire sauce, salt, and mustard. Let simmer 25 to 30 minutes. Add soy sauce, brown sugar, cayenne pepper to taste, chili powder, and garlic powder. Simmer 15 to 20 minutes more.

This basting sauce is certainly one of our favorites. Nothing fancy, just the common seasonings you usually have on hand. Can be made up ahead of time and stored in a covered glass jar and used when grilling ribs or chicken too . . . . . .

REBEL YELL HOT BARBECUE SAUCE

2 tablespoons olive oil

2 tablespoons instant minced onion, rehydrated

1/4 teaspoon instant minced garlic, rehydrated or garlic powder

1 cup chicken broth

1 can (8 oz.) tomato paste

2 tablespoons brown sugar

1/2 teaspoon ground allspice or black pepper

2 tablespoons water

1 can (8 oz.) tomato sauce

3 tablespoons red wine vinegar

2 tablespoons parsley flakes

1 teaspoon salt

1/2 teaspoon cayenne pepper or to taste

In a medium saucepan, heat oil. Add onion and garlic; sauté until onion is golden. Remove from heat. Add remaining ingredients; blend well. Simmer, uncovered, 15 minutes, stirring occasionally. Brush on venison while grilling. *Makes enough for 2 to 2 1/2 pounds venison. So - so - good!

PONCHO'S VENISON MARINADE

1 cup Picante or salsa

3 tablespoons chili powder

1 tablespoon onion powder

1/2 teaspoon crushed leaf oregano

1/2 teaspoon black pepper

1/2 cup vinegar

1 tablespoon brown sugar

1 1/2 teaspoons salt

1/2 teaspoon garlic powder

In a small bowl, combine all ingredients; blend well. Baste steaks, loin chops, or venisonburgers during grilling time. Recipe makes 2 cups or enough for about 2 pounds of venison.

A MISSISSIPPI BARBECUE SAUCE

1½ cups cider vinegar

4 teaspoons lemon juice

3 tablespoons Worcestershire sauce

2 teaspoons brown sugar

1 tablespoon liquid smoke

1 clove garlic, diced

1 cup catsup

2 teaspoons soy sauce

½ teaspoon black pepper

1 teaspoon cayenne pepper

6 oz. tomato puree

¾ teaspoon salt

1 tablespoon prepared mustard

1 cup chili sauce

Mix all ingredients in a small sauce pan and heat to boiling. Then simmer for 15 minutes. A flavorful sauce to use when grilling any venison. Venison taken north or south is most juicy and tender grilled medium rare or pink in the middle. Since venison is so lean, over grilling will dry it out.

DAD'S VENISON SAUCE

1 cup sliced mushrooms

½ cup onion, chopped

2 garlic cloves, diced

2 tablespoons butter

3-4 teaspoons flour

½ teaspoon each salt and pepper

1½ cups heavy cream

2 teaspoons lemon juice

2 teaspoons steak or soy sauce

3 teaspoons grape jelly

¼ to ½ cup water

In a frying pan over medium heat, sauté mushrooms, onion, and garlic in butter 3 to 4 minutes. Add flour, salt, and pepper and slowly add cream, stirring until blended and thickened. Add lemon juice, steak or soy sauce, jelly, and water for desired consistency. Stir, cook 1 to 2 minutes. Pour over venison steaks or burgers and serve.

RED-EYE BARBECUE SAUCE

1½ cups ketchup or chili
  sauce
1 cup black coffee
¼ cup brown sugar, or to
  taste

1 teaspoon chives
3 tablespoons cider vinegar
2 tablespoons olive oil
1 teaspoon parsley
1 teaspoon garlic powder

In sauce pan mix all ingredients. Bring to a boil, stirring to dissolve sugar. Simmer, stirring, to thicken slightly, 5 to 10 minutes. Let cool. Cover; refrigerate. Use as marinade or basting sauce. Makes 2¾ cups.

BUCKY'S WINE MARINADE

2 cups dry red wine, Rosé or
  Burgundy
1 cup water
1 rib celery, chopped
2 cloves garlic, crushed
½ teaspoon black pepper

1 cup wine vinegar
1 carrot, chopped
1 medium onion, chopped
1 tablespoon Italian
  seasoning
1 teaspoon chili powder

In a medium bowl, combine all ingredients; blend well. Place game, such as venison, in a large container. Pour marinade over meat. Cover and refrigerate 4-6 hours or overnight. Makes enough marinade for up to 4 pounds of venison.

*Option: Use 2 pounds of venison in half the marinade and save half in a container in refrigerator for next venison barbecue.

VENISON STEAK LOVERS OWN BARBECUE SAUCE

2 bottles (5 oz. size) steak
   sauce
1 cup red wine
1 teaspoon garlic powder
1 teaspoon ground black
   pepper
1/2 teaspoon liquid smoke
   seasoning

1/2 cup butter
4 tablespoons molasses
2 teaspoons cornstarch
4 tablespoons water
1/2 teaspoon cayenne pepper

In a medium-size saucepan, combine steak sauce, wine, garlic powder, black pepper, liquid smoke, butter, and molasses. Heat, stirring, until butter melts and mixture comes to a boil. Reduce heat
to very low and simmer uncovered for 15 minutes.

In a small cup, blend cornstarch and water until smooth. Stir in
cayenne pepper. Add cornstarch mixture to saucepan and cook,
stirring, until sauce boils and thickens. Cook one minute longer.

Great for steaks, chops, and venisonburgers. Store any leftover
sauce in refrigerator. Makes 2 cups.

VENISON IN HOT HERB MARINADE

1/4 cup lemon juice
1/2 cup vegetable oil
1/4 cup medium picante sauce
1/2 teaspoon sugar
1 teaspoon salt
1/4 teaspoon thyme leaf,
   crushed

1/4 teaspoon basil leaf,
   crushed
1/2 teaspoon red pepper flakes
1 teaspoon dry mustard
1 teaspoon garlic salt
1/2 teaspoon Italian seasoning
1 bay leaf
1 pound venison steak

In a bowl, combine lemon juice and oil; blend well. Add remaining
ingredients; blend well. Place venison in a shallow pan or in a double
plastic bag. Pour marinade over venison. Cover or seal. Refrigerate
4-5 hours, turning occasionally. Grill venison steaks or burgers as
you like them, basting with marinade, but do not over cook. Makes
one cup.

*T*his makes 6 plus cups of barbecue sauce. Save out the amount of sauce you will need to grill your venison steaks or roast and keep left over sauce in a sealed container for future grilling or oven broiling occasions later on. This sauce is so good you may want to use it as a venison steak dip after it is cooked. Honest, venison is at its juicy savory best grilled or broiled to medium rare or at least pink in the middle.

Carolina Style Venison BBQ Sauce

1 cup bell pepper, diced

1 cup green onions, diced

4 cups of a good store bought barbecue sauce

3 tablespoons Worcestershire sauce

4 tablespoons spicy mustard

1/2 cup brown sugar

2 tablespoons chopped parsley

2 tablespoons Italian seasoning

2 tablespoons basil flakes

1 tablespoon chili powder

1/2 teaspoon black pepper

1/2 cup water

Combine above ingredients in a medium sauce pan and simmer 20 to 25 minutes, stirring to blend. Baste venison steaks or burgers while grilling, also. Serve "hot" on the dinner table. Pass the barbecue beans please.

MARK'S BARBECUE SAUCE

1/3 cup packed brown sugar	1 cup catsup
2-3 garlic cloves, diced	1 teaspoon spicy mustard
1/3 cup red wine vinegar	1/2 teaspoon chili powder
1 teaspoon paprika	3 tablespoons Worcestershire sauce
1/2 teaspoon salt	
1 medium onion, thinly sliced	2 tablespoons lemon juice
1 cup beer	2 tablespoons cornstarch

In a medium saucepan, combine all your ingredients except corn starch. Bring to boiling over medium heat, stirring frequently. Reduce heat and cook 10 minutes, stirring often. Remove about 1/4 cup of sauce from pan. Stir cornstarch into reserved sauce until dissolved. Return to pan; blend well. Cook and stir 2 to 3 minutes or until thickened. Brush on venison while grilling. And it can be served on the table over venison.

FOOD FOR THOUGHT GRILLING TIP:

THE WISE USE OF VENISON SAUCES

What we like to do, after taking the time to prepare a venison basting sauce of ours, is to pour out an amount of sauce that we think we'll need for grilling, smoking, baking, or oven broiling for that amount of venison.

Set remaining sauce aside to be used one of two ways. One, heat it in a small pan and serve over thinly sliced venison steak or roast at meal time. Two, add to the remaining sauce in the pan thinly sliced, small pieces of venison and simmer on low heat about 30 minutes. Then enjoy or save that saucy venison to pour over rice at another meat. So, so good . . . .

Deer Hunters Know

*A*fter over two years of reading hunting related articles in over a half dozen outdoors magazines, we carefully chose what we felt were some of the most over all informative and thought provoking articles to reprint by permission in Quality Venison II.

Our objective here is to give our readers of all ages and experiences a variety of entertaining reading and the opportunity to have in one place expert advice on subjects like the easiest way to field dress your next deer, why "Meat Hunting" was and still is OK, and "First Deer" describes the hunt and the feelings a father shares with his son after he takes his first buck.

The "Moment of Truth" discusses the importance of preparing yourself mentally and physically to do everything right when it comes time for taking that all-important first shot at a whitetail deer. "Best Shot at Big Game" shares valuable tips on carefully aiming at the whitetail's vital heart, lung, liver area for that all-important first shot. Then "After the Shot" is written giving twelve logical steps for recovering your whitetail and its nutritious and delicious venison. Good reading.....indeed.!

MEAT HUNTING IS OKAY!

For many hunters, game meat is the best trophy of all

By Jim Zumbo

My 17-year old daughter, Angie, and I slowly closed in on a bunch of elk last fall. There were about 80 animals in the herd, including several bulls. We were about 200 yards out when a small group of cows spotted us. Angie quickly rested her rifle on shooting sticks, made herself comfortable in deep snow and touched off a shot. Moments later, a fat cow lay still.

Angie had a cow tag, and if you think she was disappointed because she couldn't shoot a bull, you're wrong. This was a meat hunt, pure and simple. Our family serves game meat exclusively at home and the flesh of cow elk is rated absolutely tops on our kitchen table.

A friend of ours had a bull tag for the same year. He's a good hunter, has good horses and spent plenty of time riding the elk-rich mountains of northwestern Wyoming. He passed at least 50 bulls, looking for a giant, and ended up empty-handed when the season closed. Later he admitted that he shouldn't have been so fussy. Not only did he fail to get the big bull, but he had no elk meat to show for hundreds of hours spent in the saddle. His intention was to take *any* legal bull the last day but, as often happens, he didn't see a bull. Next year, he told me, a bull was going to wear his tag—any old bull.

I also know a number of hunters who could care less about meat. Their priority is antlers, nothing else. A mounted head on the wall is the objective of the hunt; the meat is given away.

And therein lie the three basic categories of hunters: 1) those who hunt exclusively for meat; 2) those who want meat but first hold out for an impressive animal; and 3) the pure trophy hunter. Obviously, each of us hunts for different reasons.

Unlike in fishing, catch-and-release isn't an option for hunters. If you squeeze the trigger and hit what you're shooting at, you have meat on your hands. Some species may not be edible, such as coyotes or foxes, but for the most part, the bird or animal will likely be consumed.

WHAT HUNTERS GATHER

Statistics reveal just how much meat is gathered by American hunters each year. Here are some examples: 50 million doves, 25 million rabbits and squirrels, 25 million quail, 20 million pheasants, 10 million ducks, 2 million geese and 4 million deer. To the uninformed, these figures suggest we're annihilating our wildlife. The fact is, these are *surplus* animals, part of the burgeoning populations that reproduce nicely each year and allow us to hunt at all.

With the exception of wild turkeys, which sport beards and formidable spurs, birds aren't hunted as "trophies". Birds are pursued because of all the joys associated with hunting, including dog work, decoys, calling and shooting challenges, as well as their tasty flesh.

WASTE NOT

It's the antlered animals and those that yield pelts (bears, mountain lions) that trophy hunters are interested in. Some states and Canadian provinces are creating new laws requiring hunters to keep the meat of bears na lions. In 1996, for example, Montana initiated a law, which reads: "Hunters are prohibited from wasting black bear meat unless determined to contain trichinella." (Montana provides free optional lab testing for trichinella.)

And why did this state and others come up with the notion that black bear meat *must* be consumed? Wildlife officials claim that not only is bear meat palatable, but the bear deserves better than to be left behind in the woods for the sake of its hide. The law also goes along with other big-game requirements that prohibit waste of game meat. (Montana lions also must be consumed.)

An underlying reason, and one that officials won't freely admit, is based on a defense philosophy that answers accusations by anti-hunters that hunters pursue some animals (notably bears) for their pelts and leave the meat to rot in the woods. Of course, the meat doesn't rot but is quickly consumed by scavengers and predators, but the point, a correct one, is that the animal is targeted only for its trophy value by many individuals. Some hunters, by the way, hunt bear for their meat as well as their hides. (I happen to be one of them.) Mandatory laws that require hunters to keep bear meat quiet those who make a case out of it.

Most states take a dim view of wasting game meat and have laws prohibiting such waste. Alaska is probably the most strict. A serious violation in that state can lead to a jury trial. Regulations specifically say: "You must salvage all of the edible meat of moose, caribou, sheep, mountain goats, wild reindeer, deer, elk, bison or musk ox, and small-game birds for which seasons and bag limits exist." The rules also define specifically what edible meat is, and go on to prohibit the transportation of antlers *before* the meat is delivered to a pickup site. In other words, if you take a Dall's sheep and bring the horns out on the first trip with the intention of returning for the meat, you could be in very serious trouble with the law if you're caught. And rightly so.

I'm a hearty supporter of eating wild game and have a fetish against leaving any in the field (my wife calls it a phobia). I hunted turkeys in seven states this past spring, for example, and collected all the wings, thighs and drumsticks from other hunters who wanted only the breasts. With literally 40 pounds of meat that would have been tossed, I put my large pressure cooker to work and quickly had several quarts of fabulous canned turkey ready for soup and chowder this winter.

DON'T KNOCK IT

One of my biggest hunting turnoffs is the hunter who ridicules so-called "meat hunters". Disparaging comments about folks who literally hunt for venison make me sick. Luckily, most hunters don't have this attitude, which is a good thing. The non-hunting public holds the meat hunter in far higher esteem than the one who hunts solely for antlers. A Yale study conducted by Dr. Stephen Kellert found that 80 percent of Americans approve of meat hunting, while 60 percent *do not* approve of hunting for recreation or sport.

Don't make the mistake of dismissing these non-hunters as being unimportant in the battle to retain our hunting rights. Remember that they're in the majority – and they vote. Unfortunately, hunting is being challenged more and more in the ballot box these days.

I'm not against trophy hunting. I'm a professional member of the Boone and Crockett Club, and have myself passed up many animals because they didn't meet my expectations. On the other hand, I'm equally happy with a doe deer or a cow elk. I'm not above shooting a forkhorn buck or spike bull elk, either.

It riles me when I hear the old statement by animal rights people that "Americans don't need to hunt any more, since the grocery store can provide all the meat we want." I beg your pardon. There are millions of Americans who count on venison as a necessary supplement to their food budget. In some poverty-stricken areas of the South where deer limits are generous, for example, many folks rely on venison to get by. My good friends Harold Knight (a call manufacturer and outstanding hunter) and General Chuck Yeager were both raised in families where hunting was a necessity to stay alive.

Here's yet another thought on the subject, and one I've never heard or seen discussed. Yes, it's true that most of us can fulfill our meat requirements at the supermarket, but we *aren't buying venison*. Those of us who *prefer* venison must hunt it or beg it from a hunting acquaintance.

EATING HEALTHY

Venison tastes like venison, not like beef or pork. By the way, as defined by the dictionary, venison is not exclusively deer meat. *Webster's* calls it "edible flesh of a wild animal taken by hunting." *Random House* defines it as "flesh of a deer or similar animal as used for food." It's far healthier than other meats – having less fat, saturated fat and calories. It also has more protein and HDL, the "good" cholesterol, as opposed to LDL, the "bad" cholesterol which is predominately in beef and pork. Venison also has no added steroids, antibiotics or vaccines as livestock products do.

It's politically correct these days to tell people we don't necessarily hunt to kill something, but to enjoy the outdoors. I basically agree with that, and when we *do* bring home the game, it's the healthiest food you can put on your table.

 THE SKINNY ON GAME MEAT

Type of Meat	Fat	Saturated Fat	Calories	Protein
Deer	3.2g	1.2g	158	30.2g
Elk	1.9g	0.7g	146	30.2g
Antelope	2.7g	1.0g	150	29.4g
Lean Roast Beef	14.3g	5.7g	239	27.0g
Lean Ham	5.8g	1.9g	153	24.8g
Salmon	5.8g	1.4g	163	24.5g
Chicken Breast*	3.5g	1.1g	163	31.5g

*roasted, no skin
Source: U.S. Department of Agriculture (for 3.5 ounce portions)
Outdoor Life, November, 1998

Buck Deer Do Grow a New Set Every Year

THE MAGIC OF DEER ANTLERS
By Stanley E. Forbes,
Game Biologist, Pennsylvania Game Commission

It is amazing how many sportsmen still do not believe that buck deer shed and grow new antlers every year. It is true that this is a very unusual phenomenon, but magic or not, it happens!

Why does a buck lose his antlers? I have heard many hunters describing this in the field during the hunting season. One of the most popular misconceptions seems to be that the antlers are shed after the first prolonged cold spell, a spell so severe that the antlers freeze and drop off. If this is true, why don't all males shed at the same time? Obviously this is not the case; many retain their antlers well into late winter. Remember when you heard of that six- or eight-point buck seen in February, or perhaps March? Did you ever see a "spike" them? Why not?

We don't have all the answers for why antlers are shed and when, but we have a few leads. Much work has been done on the growth of antlers, and several interesting facts have come to light as by-products of these investigations.

Speaking of light, this has much to do with the growth and, we suspect, the loss of antlers. It has been pointed out by many workers dealing with the biology of deer that antler growth is what might be termed as a "secondary sex characteristic".

The early antler grown in spring is stimulated by slight changes in the activity of glands responsible for secreting male hormones. These changes are not great enough to stimulate interest in sex activity, however, even while the antler growth progresses.

As late spring and early summer approaches, the glandular changes, responsible for initiating the antler growth several months earlier, increase in tempo and effect causing the antler to attain maximum size rapidly, to harden, and to lose the velvety covering.

These body changes not only result in the animal becoming the "lordly male" of fantasy but also the "Bull of the Woods" to become more aggressive. He shows an increasing desire to engage in physical combat, although at first his desire may be satisfied by "pushing around" a few trees. This activity accounts for the "buck rubs" with which most deer hunters are familiar.

By this time, his interest in sex has become aroused, reaching its peak during the month of November. Shortly thereafter, because most of the eligible females will have been bred, his sex activity wanes; whereupon the "lordly male" loses his antlers – and his masculinity. I imagine he must feel somewhat like Samson who, when he lost his hair, lost his strength and his woman. All of these changes in the male deer have been influenced by secretions within the body as a result of glandular activity.

SHED MALES IN ANTERLESS HARVEST

The changes in glandular activity have been found to be influenced by the amount and intensity of light present during the various seasons of the year — not by temperature changes. Therefore, we can eliminate freezing as the cause of antler shedding and establish the influence of light as one of the causes, if not *the* cause. Remember, December 21, the first day of winter, is our "shortest" day of the year. It is around this time that most males start losing their racks.

Why don't all males shed their antlers at the same time? The earliest shedding dated reported in Pennsylvania has been November 27. Many sportsmen report deer with loose antlers or an antler shed during the early part of the legal deer season, but many bucks retaining antlers have been observed as late as March. The reason appears to be that as long as the adult male keeps his breeding vigor, he will retain his aantlers Here again our studies to date have pointed up the importance of a good diet. A well fed and healthy male will retain his breeding vigor longer, and in some cases, much longer, than his associates existing on an inadequate diet.

One item of interest to sportsmen is the percentage of adult males that shed both their antlers before the antlerless season. Again, we have little direct knowledge of how extensive this early shedding is, but we do have some indication. Over the past ten years, we have found that during the antlerless seasons the percentage of bucks has averaged about two per cent of the annual harvest, the extremes being 1.1 percent and 2.9 percent. This is the percentage of shed bucks found during hunting season examinations by Game Commission personnel. If these percentages are applied to the total antlerless harvest as reported by sportsmen at the close of the season, we find that 400 to 1,000 adult males or "shed bucks" are harvested during the special season. By comparing these numbers to the estimated adult male population prior to the hunting season, only about 0.8 percent of all adult males lose their racks prior to the antlerless season.

Eventually, each winter, to all elusive males that escape the hunter during the antlered season, the inevitable happens — he becomes JUST ANOTHER DEER. However, there must be comfort in knowing that there will be another year — and a new and perhaps more beautiful rack to display.

(Pitman-Robertson Project W-48-R: The White-tailed Deer Study.)

Reprinted from PENNSYLVANIA GAME NEWS
Available from the Bureau of Information & Education, Dept. AR,
Pennsylvania Game Commission, 2001 Elmerton Avenue, Harrisburg, PA 17110-9797
Publishing paid for with Game Commission funds

An Equal Opportunity Employer

Family Hunting

FIRST DEER

By John Sloan,
North American Hunting Club

The boy awoke early. It wasn't surprising that he was up before the alarm went off. He had been so excited about his first deer hunt that he hadn't slept much all night.

He pulled on his long johns and wool socks and padded to the kitchen. His father was sitting at the table, obviously working on his second helping of coffee and biscuits.

The boy poured a glass of milk and quickly buttered four biscuits. He knew he would have trouble eating; he wanted to go hunting. His father blew across his coffee cup and smiled.

"You ready, Son? It's going to be a great day. I notice we had a touch of frost last night. That's always good for deer hunting; gets them up and moving with first light," he said.

The boy was more than ready. All night he had been going over everything he had learned in hunter education, and most of the night he had been seeing huge bucks with wide racks.

"Go on and get finished dressing," his father said. "It's time we were heading for the woods. It'll be light in an hour."

The boy quickly finished dressing, but paid special attention to tying his new hunting boots. He checked to make sure he had his orange vest and hat and a box of cartridges for the old Winchester.

As he came into the kitchen his father was casing the battered and scarred Model 94. "This is your rifle now, Son," he said. "It'd do well for you to keep in mind that you have to handle it safely and responsibly or I'll have to take it away from you until you're old enough to treat it with respect."

"Yes sir," the boy said. "I'll take real good care of it and clean it every day and I'll be real careful with it, too."

As man and boy left the house and climbed into the old hunting truck, there was still no sign of light in the sky. The boy knew they were going to a piece of private property that belonged to one of his father's friends. His father had been scouting and bowhunting there quite a bit in the last two weeks. The boy felt sure that his father had seen a lot of deer there, although he had not said so.

The old heater clattered and whined and just barely put a feeble trickle of warm air around their feet, as they drove down the winding blacktop road. The boy dreamed of a buck. His dad had told him that it would be fine, even good if he killed a doe for his first deer. But no 13-year old dreams of shooting a doe.

His father finally swung the truck off the hard road onto a gravel track that led to an abandoned farm house. He stopped in front of the locked gate and parked under a giant maple tree.

The boy knew they were the only ones who had permission to hunt here, and the gate, covered with posted signs, reassured him he would be alone.

"Son, it's pretty cold this morning, but the walk up the ridge will warm you right away. I don't want you to put on your jacket until you get to your tree. That way you won't be all sweaty when you climb up. Be sure you have your orange on and take this flashlight. Make sure your rifle is unloaded and follow right behind me. We'll try to slip in quietly."

The boy slung the rifle, and his father took the climbing treestand. They began the climb up the timbered ridge. He tried to walk quietly, but it seemed that every step was on a twig or dry leaf.

At the top of the ridge, his father swung a few yards left and stopped next to an old fence that was down in several places. "Listen close," his father whispered, "I know you know how to use the climbing stand, and I've checked to make sure it is A-OK. I don't want you to go over 10 to 12 feet high. That's plenty high enough to see well, and it's more important to sit still. Here is your safety belt and your haul line. I'll put the stand on the tree and get you started."

The boy nodded even though he knew his father couldn't see him in the dark. He had been practicing with the stand on a tree in the backyard and felt comfortable using it. He had also shot more than five boxes of ammunition through the gun at the range and could put five shots through and 8-inch circle at 100 yards. He knew how to load the rifle and handle it safely.

His dad quickly hung the stand and seat climber on a straight white oak on the edge of a cedar thicket. "This is it, Son," he said, "I've been watching deer here for three weeks. They come out of the cedars and feed under those oaks yonder. You'll be able to see the trees as soon as it gets light. It's about 50 yards to the edge of the cedars and 40 to the oaks. You should be in good shape to shoot from here.

"I'll want you to face toward those cedars; just where they point out. The deer will probably show up at that spot, but you keep your eyes peeled in all directions. Just turn your head slowly from time to time. And try not to fidget in your stand. Sit still.

"If you see a deer, don't jump up and start shooting. Pick a spot and take your time. Try to raise the gun when the deer has its head down or is looking away from you. Pick a spot, just behind the shoulder and squeeze the trigger; just as you do at the range. Then, no matter what happens, sit down. Take time to calm down and then be sure to unload your rifle before you lower it down.

"Well, Son, it's up to you now. Be sure to fasten your safety belt and load your rifle carefully. Be sure to keep the hammer on half-cock until you are ready to shoot. I'll be just a ways down the ridge. If you shoot, I'll be right up. If you have trouble or need me, just holler.:

The man squeezed the boy's shoulder, "Remember, Son, killing a deer isn't the most important thing this morning. Enjoy the woods and learn from it." He resisted the urge to hug his son, turned and faded into the graying darkness.

The boy took a last look around and started to climb the tree. He stopped at what he guessed was 10 feet and tied off the safety belt. He tested the seat and platform and sat down. Quickly he pulled the rifle up and checked the muzzle to be sure it was clear. With slightly trembling hands and one dropped cartridge, he loaded the magazine and levered a round into the chamber. He checked to be sure the hammer was at half-cock and settled back against the tree.

In the dark blanket of pre-dawn, he could smell the faint hint of turpentine his father had wiped on his boots for masking scent. He listened to the calling of a horned owl and shivered a little at the slight breeze. I wish it would hurry and get light, he thought. Not that I'm scared or anything; it's just that I can see better in the light.

Slowly, he began to make out the shape of the trees around him. They began to appear ghost-like out of the landscape. Then came the outlines of rocks and logs. Little by little, the white oak ridge came alive.

When it was good light, but not yet sun-up, the boy heard a

rustling in the leaves. He strained his eyes and ears for another sound or a glimpse of the deer he knew must surely be coming his way. The rustling came again, closer this time. Suddenly the boy glimpsed a flash of gray, not 20 feet from him. The squirrel jumped off the log and raced away.

The boy relaxed and smiled at himself, trying to quiet his trembling knees. He turned his attention back to the cedar thicket and trail leading to the oaks.

"Gee," he thought, "that patch of white sure looks like a deer's ear." The white patch suddenly moved and at once became a whole deer.

The boy's breath caught, and his heart began to hammer. Had he not been so excited, he would have better been able to study the deer. He would have seen the gleam of sunlight off the forked antlers as the buck turned his head. He would have seen the other two deer in the thicket behind the buck. Both had larger antlers.

With trembling hands and shaking knees, the boy brought the rifle to full cock. He tried to pick a spot behind the shoulder. The front sight began to settle in the notch of the rear sight when the gun went off.

The boy's dad fought the urge to go running up the ridge. "I have to give him time to look for his deer or get his story ready." He smiled, took a fresh dip of snuff and began to slowly climb the ridge.

The boy was standing at the edge of the cedars. "Oh, Dad, I missed him," he yelled, barely able to keep the tears off his cheeks. "He was right there, and I missed him."

His father smiled, "Son, I reckon I missed the first deer I shot at. It's nothing to be ashamed of, but before we give up, let's take a little look around. Never say you've missed a deer until you're absolutely sure."

The boy showed his dad exactly where the deer was standing. The older hunter looked back once at the stand tree, then to the boy's surprise, moved several feet farther away from the cedars. He paused, bending to look closely at the ground.

"Come here, Son," he said. "See the way the ground is all scuffed up and the way the leaves are scattered and turned over? Here's where you deer was standing. When a deer is hit, many times it will tear the ground up some. Maybe you didn't miss."

The man began to work back toward the cedars, moving slowly and studying the ground. "A hit deer will often run back the way it came. They know it is safe where they just came from," the man said. "Another thing. A deer has four legs. When they run, one of them has to hit the ground. See the way those leaves are turned over? He went that way."

"But there's no blood," said the boy.

"Even the hardest hit deer don't always bleed right away. That's why you have to look really good."

"Did I hit this deer, Dad?"

"Maybe you did and maybe you didn't," he said. "You smell anything, Son?"

"No sir."

"Sure you do," the man said. "You smell wood smoke from that house across the road. You smell the rotting leaves. You smell the hint of winter. You smell the cedars. You smell a lot of things. You just don't know how to recognize them yet."

"You see a lot, too. You see squirrels and woodpeckers, wrens and chipmunks, leaves falling and turning colors, jet vapors in the sky and beams of sunlight coming through the trees. It's all here. You just have to take time to look and learn. See, that's what deer hunting is all about. It's not just about killing a deer.

"Come here, Son. Look at that dead treetop yonder. Look close."

The boy ran to the fallen top and came to a skidding stop. The 4-point had fallen just on the other side in a wide patch of sunlight. "I got him, Dad! I got him!"

This time, his dad couldn't resist a hug before he helped him field dress the deer. As he wiped a slight bit of dew from the corner of his eye, he knew there was another deer hunter in the family and recalled the day, many years before, that he had killed his first deer.

Reprinted from North American Hunter November/December 1997

YOUR BEST SHOT AT BIG GAME

Hunting has changed somewhat over the past 50 years, but much remains the same. After all, firearms, ammunition, and game are still basically what they were a hundred years ago. Even with modern developments in archery equipment, it is still simply a sharp blade that really does the job.

Smart hunters still aim for the largest vital area they can see. For just about all animals, that is the heart-lung-liver area. Head and neck hits, of course can also be deadly, but there is a surprisingly large amount of space in the head and neck that may not produce a quick kill when hit with bullets or shotgun slugs. (It's just the opposite with birds and birdshot — the head is the place to aim because birdshot does not penetrate well.)

When hunting with arrows, hitting the vital heart-lung-liver area behind the shoulder is even more critical because arrows don't have any shock or "knock-down" power. Bowhunters today are well-schooled in where to aim because every licensed bowhunter in New York is a graduate of a bowhunter education course.

One key point hunters learn in the bowhunting course is that the real target is inside the animal, not on its hide. This means that hunters must compensate for the angle if the deer does not present a broadside shot. Aim farther back if the deer is quartering away, and aim higher if you are shooting from above. A good rule of thumb is to aim just above the elbow of the OPPOSITE side of the deer.

With firearms, the target is the same, but with a bigger margin for error, because the shoulder, with large bones that can stop arrows, is another good place to hit. The shoulder bones make shots with arrows fruitless if the deer is quartering toward the bowhunter.

Play the odds. Which target do you have a better chance of hitting? The softball size brain area; the narrow baseball size neck vertebrae hidden somewhere in the neck; or the heart-lung-liver area as big as a soccer ball? Whether you are a gambler or not, the biggest target is the best.

After the Shot...recovering your deer

12 STEPS TO RECOVERING YOUR DEER

The sound of the shot startles the deer into flight. To the inexperienced hunter this may be disappointing but experienced hunters watch the flight of the deer with intense concentration and anticipation. These hunters know that after a well-placed shot, a running deer is often the beginning of the end of the hunt. All hunters try for a quick, clean kill, but many don't realize that quick and clean does not always mean instantly.

Many fatally wounded deer immediately run, especially when hit in the largest vital zone — the heart-lung-liver area just behind the shoulder. I have taken several deer that obviously had no idea they were hit, but were startled, and took off like a race horse out of the starting gate. In bowhunting season, some deer will run a short distance and resume feeding for several seconds until blood loss causes them to black out. That won't happen after the thunder of a gunshot. During the regular season, deer often collapse on the run.

Never assume you missed. Most well placed shots will put a deer down in a few seconds, but deer can travel hundreds of yards in that time. If there is no snow to clearly show you the tracks, it may take a while to find the deer. Here are some step-by-step hints to make the task easier.

1. Don't move. Keep quiet and follow the deer with your eyes and ears.

2. Mark your location before you move. Remember exactly where the deer was standing when you shot, and also the last place you saw it. Take compass readings if necessary. Mark these two places also. Tissues make good markers (not white ones, for safety reasons) as well as surveyor's flagging. Make sure you pick them up later.

3. At the point of impact, deer hair and possible blood will help confirm where the arrow or slug hit. (Bowhunters should look beyond where the deer stood to see if the arrow passed through the body. Hair and body fluids on the arrow will provide clues for your search. If you can't find the arrow, assume it is in the deer.) Evidence here will help you decide whether to follow immediately or to get your hunting partners for help. If you find stomach contents or intestinal fluids, for instance, wait at least a couple of hours — preferably more — to avoid pushing the deer farther.

4. Look for drops of blood, tracks, or scuff marks. Mark your trail, especially where you find evidence that the deer passed. Don't step on the signs you were following – you may want to check them later.

5. While you are trailing, be slow and quiet, as though you were stalking a live deer. In fact, you may be doing just that, so keep looking ahead for the deer, not just at signs on the ground.

6. Blood may not always be on the ground. Look for blood on trees, grass and other plants at the height of the wound. Don't be discouraged if there isn't much blood. Some wounds cause internal hemorrhaging that puts the deer down just as fast as external bleeding.

7. If you are tracking on dry leaves, and it's windy, you may have to turn leaves over if the blood trail is sparse. It's easier if you pay special attention to rocks, logs, and tree roots – things that don't blow away.

8. Look for details. Drops hitting the ground may splash, making small "fingers" pointing in the direction of travel.

9. Blood is hard to spot on leaves that are already red. You can look for the shine, feel it, or rub it with a tissue to detect blood.

10. Some surfaces soak up blood so it doesn't look red. Use drug store hydrogen peroxide or commercial blood detectors that foam when they contact blood.

11. If you lose the trail, don't give up. A systematic search often works. The "increasing L" system works well. Pace off a straight line, make a right turn and pace off the same distance to complete the first "L". Keep turning right, increasing the distance after each two lines.

12. When you find your deer, it's eyes will be open if it is dead. Approach it from the back, and touch the eye with a stick to make sure.

Congratulations! Now it's time to fill out your tags and field dress the deer.

—Wayne Jones, Sportsman Education Administrator

Reprinted from *Wild In New York*, Fall 1998

Much more detail is available in pocket-size booklets from the National Bowhunter Education Foundation, 249-B E. 29th St., #503, Loveland, CO 80538 Phone 970-635-1994. Also on the Worldwide Web at www.nbef.org.

Big Game Recovery Guide (18 pp.) $2.00, Tree Stand Guide (40 pp.) $2.00; Shot Placement Guide (24pp.) $2.00; or all three under one cover in the NBEF Responsibility Guide, $5.00

Hunting Guns, Ammo and Optics

THE MOMENT OF TRUTH
By Bill Miller

When it coms to shotgunning, there are two kinds of choke I'm familiar with. The first is the kind of choke that happens when they start the "North American Outdoors" or "The Shooting Sports" camera rolling and I'm supposed to hit those shrinking clay targets on every single shot.

The second kind of choke in wing-shooting is the constriction of the shotgun's barrel near the muzzle which controls the spread and density of the pattern it throws. You know, the ones we constantly change hoping in some way that selecting the right tube will make up for the previous kind of choke!

Well, normally in North American Hunter's "Hunting Guns, Ammo and Optics" column you'd expect to read about the intricacies of the latter kind of choke, but not this time around. With the opening of most 1997–98 firearms whitetail seasons either imminent or in your very recent history, it's important that every hunter revisits his or her preparation for the moment of truth.

Though in a pure calculation of days, hours, minutes and seconds the shooting of a deer or any other game animal is probably the smallest portion of the hunt, it is what makes hunting hunting. The real reward for the months of anticipation, the days of preparation and the hours of waiting is the adrenalin rush of having within your killing range an animal that meets your personal requirements for harvest.

Amonth the North American Hunting Club membership, I'm pretty certain that excitement at the moment of truth is unanimous. Certainly the feeling itself is as individual as each of the nearly 800,000 members in the Club, but every hunter's case is generated by the adrenalin rush that is part and parcel of being a predator. In the animal kingdom it's what allows a lioness to attack a water buffalo twice her size or wolves to brave the flailing hooves of a cow moose defending her calf.

So for a predator, this surge of excitement is a good thing, in fact, an essential thing to its survival. That's the reason "the rush" is a desirable, sought-after sensation to human hunters, though we're far removed from counting on it for sheer continuation of our existence. But like many "good things" it can be too much for human hunters to handle. When the excitement takes over, hunters experience what is commonly known as buck fever.

It's called "buck fever" because the over-excitement is most common in hunting deer — North America's most popular big game animal. But buck fever can strike any kind of hunter at any time, and while it's more likely to hit the less experienced hunter, none of us can claim to be fever-free.

I blame to fever for the antics of hunters who cannot sit still while the geese are making their legs-down approach or while the gobbler is in full strut just 10 yards beyond good shotgun range. At those moments, with the adrenal gland and the heart pumping in sequence, every instinct is tell you to pounce, to take action. It's only reason and experience that allow us to keep in check what our primal instincts are demanding that we do.

However, there are lots of North American hunting guides and African professional hunters who can tell you endless stories of where that line is crossed when the game is brown bear, polar bear, Cape Buffalo or leopard! Make that sheer terror when you have to go into the brush after an animal that might be less than dead!

It falls on the shoulders of ever North American Hunting Club member to prepare himself or herself for the moment of truth as best as he or she can. Like seemingly everything else in hunting, that means practice well ahead of heading into the woods. If you are troubled by buck fever in any type of hunting situation, you can prepare yourself by daydreaming daily about that particular moment of truth.

Today let's set the scene at a Texas tower shooting house. My Magnum Research Mountain Eagle in .280 Rem. with its Simmons Aetec scope set on 6X is leaned in the corner to my right, cartridges in the magazine, bolt half-open. On the small shelf underneath the window in front of me are my binoculars. Clamped in the right edge of that open window is my spotting scope. In the corner to

WAYS TO PREVENT BUCK FEVER

• Visualize your upcoming hunts. Try to work in every variable so that when that trophy comes into view, you can go into auto-pilot.

• Review the annual "You Call The Shots" features in North American Hunter magazine. Try to put yourself under the same mental stress you'll face when you really see those animals, then compare your analysis to the experts.

• Create your own "You Call The Shots" scenarios when you're watching nature shows on television. They're a great second-best when you can't be in the field.

• Get in good physical condition before your hunts. It's tought to fend off buck fever if you aren't on top of your game all the way around.

my left is my daypack. Its zipper is open so I can silently reach for any of the content.

It's 10 minutes into legal shooting time. I'm straining to make out detail in the forms of deer that are already moving inside the edge of the bushline.

There! One stepped in the clear. It's a...doe. There's another. Wait, that last one's a buck, but just a spike.

Hmmm...what's going on? They're all looking down the sendero to my right. I s-l-o-w-l-y turn my head to look out the window on that end of the house.

There's a big-bodied animal in the brush. Wait — there are cattle out here too; is it a cow? No, it's a deer... a good buck.

I watch him without moving until he leaves my view at the corner of the blind. Last I saw him, he was walking stiff-legged toward a group of deer in the wide aprt of the sendero. I reach for the rifle, slide the bolt back and ease a shell into the chamber as the muzzle is slowly going through the opening.

The buck's not coming. Where'd he go?

A sideways glance out the right window reveals that he has turned back to check on another deer in his path. The two meet. It's another small buck that he quickly chases away. Then he turns and trots toward the feeding deer again.

At the edge of the wide opening, he pauses behind a mesquite. All I can see is his silhouette behind the branches in the growing light. It seems like an eternity that he stands surveying the feeding animals.

Finally he steps into the open. The guide who dropped me off told me that patch of prickly pear is 123 yards from the tower, so the buck is about 150.

OK, here we go. The crosshairs waver, then I catch my breath and they settle in the crease behind the front shoulder. I squeeze the trigger and...

The moment of truth is over.

This kind of mental practice is critical to the success of your hunts...and it's a whole lot of fun. Let's see, now I think I'll head to Montana for that elk trip I've got coming up in a few weeks. I've been on the mountain all day. The temperature has been dropping, and there's a little snow in the air. The park I'm watching is covered in elk tracks...

Oh, while I'm gone...feel free to daydream about your own upcoming trip. If you boss catches your, tell you're just practicing to better handle your job stress.

Reprinted from North American Hunter

Private Lessons

14 STEPS TO A WELL-DRESSED DEER
You don't even have to roll up your sleeves
By Terry Sullivan

THE NECESSITIES
- **A good, sharp pocket-knife (large hunting knives look better than they work and are awkward to use)**
- **Rope to hang the carcass**
- **A cheesecloth bag to cover the carcass**
- **A heavy cotton or canvas bag to transport the meat**

The best way to field-dress big game was developed by Nevada hunter Smokey Baird. Old Smokey has killed at least one deer every year since he was 12, or about four dozen to date. What Smokey did was to make sure someone was with him when he got his deer. Sometimes it was a stranger, sometimes a friend. Once the deer was killed, Old Smokey would scratch his head, look dumb and say something like, "Shucks, I've gutted a few of these deer, but I never really got the hang of it. Do you think you could show me how you do it?"

This method worked on one of his best friends three years running. And it always worked on strangers. No one really wanted to gut Old Smokey's deer, but they couldn't pass up the chance to show off.

Perhap's Smokey's technique will work for you this fall. But in the event that it doesn't, try the following methods of field-dressing and caring for game, including deer, elk, antelope and sheep. If you don't, the result could be tainted meat; if you do, you'll be serving delectable meals this winter.

1. Punch your deer tag. It's illegal to kill a deer without a tag. The tag must be with the animal at all times.

2. Turn the animal so its head is pointing downhill. If the ground is flat, just drape its rear end across a bush. (If you intend to have your trophy mounted, do not perform steps 3 and 4 at this point.)

3. Slit the throat just below the jawbone to bleed the animal.

4. Sever the windpipe — which is the firm, hollow white tube.

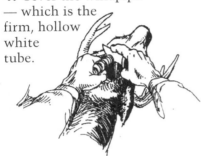

5. While the hindquarters are elevated and the animal is being bled, sever and discard the testicles.

6. Remove the scent glands located on each rear leg near the knee joint. These glands are easily identified by the hair protruding from them. Cut well beyond the direct gland areas to make sure no part remains. (Some folks think this step is unnecessary, so you may want to skip it, buck Clay Baird, Smokey's son, says it is imperative to remove these glands. He even uses a different knife so that he doesn't taint any other part of the animal. Clay has killed and dressed more deer than most hunters and he is a connoisseur of good meat, so suit yourself on this one.)

7. Very carefully cut a circle around the anus so that it is completely free of any connecting skin. Do not puncture the intestines. If you do, the meat's good flavor can be substantially altered.

8. Turn the animal on its back with its hindquarters downhill.

9. Cut the penis free all the way to the anus so that both parts will be free to move into or out of the previously cut circle. Do not remove yet.

10. Your next step is to open the stomach cavity. Hold the back of your knife blade against your index finger. Start your cut at about the point where you began cutting the genitals free, sliding your finger and blade just under the skin. Be extremely careful to cut only the skin, leaving all organs intact to avoid tainting the meat. Cut all the way to the rib cage.

11. Cut through the ribs at the breastbone all the way to the neck. If your pocketknife is properly sharpened, you'll have no trouble at all. (You should eliminate this step if you plan to take the carcass out on a pack animal because the rib cage provides good support.)

12. Connected to the rib cage and extending to the spine is a thick skin called the diaphragm, which

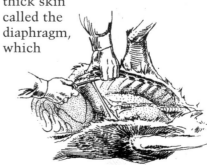

separates the stomach from the chest cavity. Trim this loosely from the carcass.

13. Spread the rib cage, and with your free hand, grasp the windpipe above the lungs and pull downward. Remember, you severed the windpipe earlier. (If you did not cut the throat previously, you will need to reach up into the chest cavity as far as you can now to cut the windpipe.) By this time, everything — including the anus and penis — should be sliding toward the rear and over the pelvis. All the innards should exit through the stomach opening. If you missed anything, you can find it easily now and carefully trim it loose.

14. If there is a tree nearby, hang the animal by its head and let it drain completely. Wipe all blood and foreign material out of the cavity with clean rags. If there is no tree, prop the animal on a rock or bush.

From the innards, separate the liver, heart, and any other organ you like to eat. Place in bags to keep clean and store in the coolest available place.

You have now finished field dressing your animal. Don Swindlehurst of Wildhorse, Nevada, is one of the Great Basin's best hunters. "After you've prepped your game, your hands will be wet, but for the most part there should be no blood or mess," he says. "If you did it properly, you should not even have to roll up your sleeves."

Illustrations by Dimitry Schidlovsky

GETTING ON THE ROAD

Now it's time to figure out how to get the carcass back to camp. The least desirable method is dragging, but if this is necessary, you should tie the cavity tightly so no dirt can enter. Should you not intend to take out at once, leave your animal hanging in the shade with the cavity propped open to allow air to circulate freely. In treeless areas, position the carcass in the coolest spot you can find, making absolutely sure it's out of direct sunlight.

If you feel strong enough to carry your trophy back to camp, it's a simple matter to make a slit in the space between the tendon and ankle on each rear leg and put one front leg through each slit. You have now created a "backpack" through which you can slip one arm and your head and return to camp. You'll be carrying the animal with the head up, so be sure you cover any antlers or horns with light cloth to completely hide them. Hunters have been shot at for failing to take this precaution.

SAVING YOUR HIDE

The sooner you get the carcass back to camp the better, be
cause the hide should be removed as quickly as possible —
always in the same day, preferably the same hour. Once
back at camp, remove the feet by cutting a circle all the
way to the bone at the ankle joint and breaking across
your knee as you would a piece of wood. Be sure you
cut below the tendons on the back legs as they make a
perfect loop for hanging the carcass.

To skin the deer, hang it head down so the rear
legs are at your chest level. Make a slit
down the inside of each leg to the
stomach cavity and pull (sometimes
cutting) the hide loose from the legs
and hindquarters.   You can now
raise the animal higher and continue
to pull or cut the hide all the way down
to the neck. You will also have to slit down
the inside of each front leg. The head and hide
can now be severed from the carcass by
continuing the cut previously made at the throat.
(For mounting, skin as close to the head as possible and
then cut the neck loose from the skin, leaving head and hide
together.)

Roll the hide up with the head. In most states, it is illegal
not to bring out the head and hide with the carcass. Also, switch
the tag to the meat if you had previ-
ously tied it to an antler or horn.
Completely cover the carcass with a
cheesecloth bag, leaving no opening
for insects, and hang it in the coolest
place possible.

Transport your animal in a dust-
proof, heavy cotton or canvas bag. The
organs you saved should be washed,
drained and placed in clean containers.
Unlike the carcass, the organs should be
put in airtight containers such as drip-
proof plastic bags.

Reprinted from *Outdoor Life* – November, 1998

Illustrations by Dimitry Schidlovsky

INDEX

Quality Venison
Homemade Recipes and Homespun Deer Tales

"More than just a cookbook, Quality Venison guides you from the instant your deer is down through all the field dressing, butchering and other steps necessary to make the finest of gourmet meals…Hunters and cooks of all levels of experience will enjoy Quality Venison."

—Bob Mitchell, Editor, Pennsylvania Game News Magazine

"Quality Venison is more than a cookbook with a pretty cover. It has brains inside to go with its good looks…The book's main aim is to take the gamy taste out of the venison. That starts when the deer is first taken, not when you are starting to prepare a meal. Loder tells you how in this field to meals cookbook."

—Gary Fallesen, Outdoors Writer, Democrat and Chronicle, Rochester, NY

A complete field to freezer guide for preparing venison that is lean, tender and not "gamy". Follow the author's instructions for preparing your venison and you're assured of great tasting meat!

You've been reading about the original *Quality Venison* cookbook in this book, and here's how to buy a copy of your very own. We don't want you to miss any of the great recipes in the first book (all are different from the recipes in *Quality Venison II*) and we know you'll enjoy the deer tales and great article reprints, so be sure to add this book to your collection.

You'll love the deer tales — straight from the author's hunting journal. The cover is a full color reproduction of wildlife artist Jack Paluh's painting, "In Thanksgiving", a reverent rendering of Native American hunters and their spiritual ties to the whitetail.

Contains 150 family tested recipes in 5 sections:
- Grilling Venison
- Italian Style
- Crockery Style
- Traditional Style
- Family Favorites

Published in 1998, 184 pages, 6 x 9, comb bound with a hard cover.

Order your copy today by using the handy order form on the facing page, or simply send $14.95 plus $3.50 shipping and handling per copy (Pennsylvania residents add $1.11 sales tax) to:

Loders' Game Publications
PO Box 1615 • Cranberry Township, PA 16066

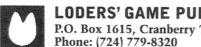

LODERS' GAME PUBLICATIONS, INC.
P.O. Box 1615, Cranberry Township, Pennsylvania 16066
Phone: (724) 779-8320

Please send _____ copies of *Quality Venison II* @ $14.95 each _____

Please send _____ copies of *Quality Venison* @ $14.95 each _____

Postage and handling @ $3.50 each _____

Pennsylvania residents, add sales tax @ $1.11 each _____

Total _____

Make checks payable to: Loders' Game Publications, Inc.

Name _____

Address _____

City _____ State _____ Zip _____

Phone (day) _____ (night) _____

☐ Please keep me informed of future wild game publications

- -

LODERS' GAME PUBLICATIONS, INC.
P.O. Box 1615, Cranberry Township, Pennsylvania 16066
Phone: (724) 779-8320

Please send _____ copies of *Quality Venison II* @ $14.95 each _____

Please send _____ copies of *Quality Venison* @ $14.95 each _____

Postage and handling @ $3.50 each _____

Pennsylvania residents, add sales tax @ $1.11 each _____

Total _____

Make checks payable to: Loders' Game Publications, Inc.

Name _____

Address _____

City _____ State _____ Zip _____

Phone (day) _____ (night) _____

☐ Please keep me informed of future wild game publications